SCOTTISH
HILL TRACKS

SCOTTISH RIGHTS OF WAY SOCIETY

Scottish Hill Tracks

A guide to hill paths, old roads and rights of way

Third Edition

Original Compilation by
D G Moir

Revised by
J C Bartholomew
D J Bennet
and
C Stone

SCOTTISH RIGHTS OF WAY SOCIETY

Published in Great Britain by The Scottish Rights of Way Society
and The Scottish Mountaineering Trust, 1995
Copyright © The Scottish Rights of Way Society

First Edition 1947
Second Edition 1975
Third Edition 1995

British Library Cataloguing in Publication Data
Scottish Hill Tracks: Guide to Hill Paths,
Old Roads and Rights of Way. – 3Rev.ed
  I. Bartholomew, John C. II. Stone,
  Clifford
  344.1103942

  ISBN 0-9502811-5-8

Produced by Scottish Mountaineering Trust (Publications) Ltd
Typeset by Westec, North Connel
Colour Separations by Par Graphics, Kirkcaldy
Printed by St Edmundsbury Press, Bury St Edmunds
Bound by Hunter and Foulis, Edinburgh

Distributed by Cordee, 3a DeMontfort Street, Leicester LE1 7HD

Acknowledgments

The Scottish Rights of Way Society acknowledges with thanks the financial assistance of the Countryside Commission for Scotland (now Scottish Natural Heritage) towards the preliminary research for this book, and the co-operation of the Scottish Mountaineering Trust in its publication.

The editors warmly acknowledge the willing help of the following in checking on the ground the majority of the routes described in this book, and notifying the changes necessary for this revision.

Ken Andrew	Bill Forsyth	William Morris
Sandy Anton	Michael Foxley	Sheila Murray
J. Bailey	Dave Holliday	Andrew Nelson
Donald Bennet	John Harvey	Ian Provan
Elizabeth Berwick	C. C. Hemmings	Derek Purdy
Andrew Buckham	R. J. Kehoe	Bert Rutherford
Irvine Butterfield	Stuart Kermack	G. Sadler
Bob Carnell	Jenny Kett	Frank Spaven
R. J. Carpenter	Alistair Lawson	Alex Sutherland
Eric Clive	John Leech	Euan Terras
Ann Cordiner	Douglas Lowe	Mrs M.Towers
Jim Cosgrove	H. McKenzie	Leen Volwerk
John Coul	Catherine MacLeod	Anne Wakeling
R. Crawford	S. F. Marriot	David Warnock
John Davidson	Janet Meikle	Adam Watson
Muriel Dymock	George Menzies	Roger Watts
Alan Fletcher	Jim Montgomery	Robin Woodger

As the co ordinating editor, I wish to record my particular thanks to Cliff Stone for his patient and steadfast support throughout the lengthy process of the revision, and also to Donald Bonnet for his indispensible contribution to the design and production of this book.

John Bartholomew

iv

Contents

Illustrations

Foreword

By Tom Weir

This handsome book, with colour photographs, maps and revised descriptions of Scottish hill tracks, old highways and drove roads, combines the two volumes, one, Southern Scotland and two, Northern Scotland by D.G.Moir, published by John Bartholomew & Son Ltd in 1947, revised in 1975, and further researched in the light of recent changes of land use.

It was Government fear of the Highlanders that sent Field Marshal George Wade to Scotland in 1724 to build military roads with the aim of pacifying the homelands of the Jacobites who had threatened the peace in 1715 and 1719. By 1739 Wade had increased his Highland companies to ten, had formed the Black Watch Regiment from clansmen loyal to the Westminster Government, and he and his successors carried forward a big programme of road building.

Thomas Telford (1757-1834), son of a Border shepherd whose genius earned him the title 'Colossus of the Roads', achieved in his lifetime more than any other single individual, pushing highways through 900 miles of mountainous and boggy terrain.

Balmoralism dates from the mid-1850s when the wealthy, made rich from the proceeds of the Industrial Revolution, were rapidly acquiring large Highland estates and building shooting lodges, bothies and well-made paths ideal for ponies and walkers.

By 1912 there were 203 deer forests occupying three and a half million acres. Cattle and sheep had been banished together with unwanted people. Owners and occupiers of these lands had become accustomed to purchasing privacy, but the introduction of the popular bicycle around 1885 brought a gentle breeze of change, coinciding as it did with the formation of the Cairngorm Club and the Scottish Mountaineering Club, just over 100 years ago.

In the Lowlands game-preserving and agriculture had gone hand in hand in the Border country with hedges, parks and coppice wood, integrating sport with farming. Walter Scott himself had channelled much of his vast earnings into tree-planting and beautifying his stretch of the Tweed.

The Reverend A.E.Robertson, first completer of all 283 Munros on the original list, was a self-reliant user of old tracks on foot and by bicycle, without which he could not have achieved his marathon in the years between 1889 and 1901. He was an eager compiler of old tracks, coffin roads and cross-country routes. He became a director of the Scottish Rights of Way Society in 1923, Chairman in 1931, and after its reorganisation became its first President in 1946 – the same year that he was elected a Fellow of the Royal Society of Edinburgh

To walk these ancient tracks demands not only sleuth work, but can be a contribution to history in noting changes and keeping this record of old routes up to date.

Introduction

This book gives route descriptions for over three hundred cross-country walks in all parts of Scotland, most of which can be accomplished in a day. The majority of these routes follow existing roads (some public and some private), tracks and footpaths. In places there are no such recognisable features, and the routes cross moors and hills where the walker must find his own way; in other places old paths and tracks may, through disuse, have returned to their natural state and now can barely be recognised as vague lines across grassy hillsides or heather moors.

Many of the routes follow ancient roads and drovers' tracks, and some are now regarded as rights of way. However, not all the routes described in this book are rights of way, and no claims are made about their legal status. However, in choosing the routes and describing their lines, the compilers have selected those where it is felt that the public can go with reasonable confidence that they are not infringing the legitimate rights and privacy of those who live in the countryside.

Although the main purpose of this book is to describe cross-country routes over open country, moors and hills, there are inevitably sections where the walker must go along public roads. The choice of routes has been made to reduce to a minimum the amount of walking on main roads with heavy traffic, but there remain many sections of walking along minor country roads which do not carry much traffic. This is inevitable and will not, it is hoped, detract from the quality of the routes as a whole.

It is to be hoped that not only will this book open the eyes of many readers to the great wealth of one-day cross-country walks in Scotland, but also stir their imagination to the possibility of any number of long-distance routes lasting several days. One has only to look at the maps at the end of this book to see that the great network of routes covering the country can be linked in literally dozens of different ways. The adventurous walker can plan his or her own personal pilgrimage across Scotland, from south to north or west to east, and thereby dispel the criticism levelled by some at the existing designated long-distance routes that they inhibit the individual's route-planning initiative and direct him along paths that have been eroded by the boots of many other walkers.

THE OLD ROADS OF SCOTLAND

Roman Roads

The oldest known roads in Scotland are those made by the Roman soldiers between AD 78 and 185. Their three main lines of road can still be seen:

1. From the Cheviots to the River Tweed at Melrose and on to the Forth.

2. From the Solway Firth up Annandale and northwards to the Lower Clyde.

3. From the Roman Wall at Camelon by Stirling and Strathearn to the River Tay north of Perth.

The best remaining section of Roman road is the 20km stretch of Dere Street from the Cheviots to Jedfoot, which has been very little disturbed since it was made in the second century. This stretch shows that the usual idea of a Roman road as being a long straight line is only partially true. The Roman engineer did prefer a direct line, sighted from skyline to skyline, but he chose his route with skill and on hilly ground found a winding road more practicable than a straight one.

Roman roads have endured because they were well constructed. Part of the Annandale road was found by excavation to have an 11-inch layer of large stones and a 4-inch layer of small stones, all bound with clay with a total width of 21 feet. The standard construction was four layers, two of stones, a third of mixed material, and a top layer, sometimes of paving stones but more generally of gravel bound with clay.

Mediaeval Roads

Some of our roads may be even older than Roman times, but we have no proof of this in Scotland. In England an extensive system has clearly been in use in prehistoric times, and there are some ridgeways in southern Scotland which may be either prehistoric or mediaeval, for example the ridgeway from Soutra to Melrose known as the Girthgate (route 38), the Minchmoor track (route 25) and the ridgeway from Peebles to Yarrow (route 22). The mediaeval traveller had the same ideas as his prehistoric ancestor. He wanted to avoid bogs, streams, ravines and forests, and he therefore climbed to the high ground as quickly as possible and kept along the ridges until he found the shortest crossing of the next valley.

The foundation of abbeys and churches, and the growth of villages and towns, resulted in the developement of more roads, particularly in the valleys where the new settlements were growing up, but for more than fourteen centuries after the Roman period there was no proper road construction in Scotland. The word "road" itself originally referred to riding, and it was not until Shakespeare's time that it was used for the road to travel on. The older name was way or highway, and in Scotland gate or gait. We find a Thirlstanegate mentioned in a charter about 1240, and there are numerous Gatesides still among our place-names.

Horseback and foot were the only means of travel in the Middle Ages, and except for waggons of a kind owned by some of the abbeys, all merchandise was carried by packhorse. For these a beaten track along the ground was sufficient, trodden out by the passage of many feet, without any made road.

In the course of time some of these tracks have been made into roads, whilst others have been left to revert to their natural state. Interesting examples are the tracks which cross the Cheviots into England (routes 1 to 11) and the old routes across the Eastern Grampians from Deeside to the south which still retain their old names – Tolmount, Capel Mounth etc (routes 166 to 176). One useful indication of an old road is when it forms a parish boundary, as most of Scotland was divided into parishes in the 12th and 13th centuries. This is not always conclusive proof that a road is quite so old, since there have been some more recent changes in parish boundaries, particularly in the 15th and 16th centuries.

Drove Roads

The rearing of cattle and sheep was for centuries the mainstay of the Highland economy, and every autumn large droves of animals were taken from the Highlands to the cattle markets or trysts. The most important market was for long the Michaelmas Tryst at Crieff, where in the course of a week as many as 30,000 cattle were sold, besides a smaller number of sheep. The chief purchasers were English, and it was not uncommon for them to hire the sellers to drive the stock on to England.

By 1770 the Michaelmas Tryst was transferred to Falkirk. In a lawsuit in 1846 evidence was given that for centuries people north of the Grampians had been in the habit of driving sheep and cattle to the southern markets along two lines of drove roads:

1. By Drumochter, Atholl and Crieff from the northern and eastern parts of Ross and Inverness-shire.

2. By Glen Coe, the Black Mount and Callander from Wester Ross, Inverness, Argyll and the Western Isles.

The drove road by Glen Coe had been in use long before the military road was made in 1750 on the line of the old road, with occasional diversions. It was the practice of the drovers to travel ten miles a day, as that was the distance the animals could go without suffering serious harm, and to rest the animals at regular stances on the roadside.

Other markets on a smaller scale were held all over Scotland. In the action brought in the Court of Session in 1887 to preserve the Glen Doll right of way (route 175) it was proved that it had for long been used by drovers taking sheep from Braemar to the market at Cullow, near Kirriemuir. The long distances travelled by drovers is shown by a report to the Privy Council in 1598 concerning McKenzie of Kintail, who had 24 cattle stolen on their way to the fair at Glamis.

Many local drove roads owe their existence to the old Highland custom of families moving in early summer with their cattle, sheep and goats to the hill shielings, where they spent the summer in stone or turf huts, making the milk into butter and cheese. This custom died out as the higher grazings were converted into sheep farms. Other drove roads were in use in fairly recent years by sheep going to and from their winter grazings. Auction marts and modern transport have ended these old customs. A few drove roads still carry the name Thieves Road as reminders of the times when cattle lifting was practised on a large scale. (See A.R.B.Haldane: *The Drove Roads of Scotland,* Nelson, 1952).

Kirk and Coffin Roads

These, as the names indicate, are local rights of way to churches and churchyards. In the Highlands many of them were quite long tracks, for example the route from Glen Lyon to Dalmally which was used by the Macgregors going from their homes in Glen Lyon to their clan burial ground at the foot of Glen Orchy. Coffins might be carried for many miles, all the local men taking turns.

Osgood Mackenzie records, in his book *A Hundred Years in the Highlands*, that when Lady Mackenzie died in 1830 five hundred men, taking turns, carried the coffin sixty miles from Gairloch to Beauly. When coffins were rested, everyone added a stone to a cairn on the spot, a custom that was responsible for many of the cairns still to be seen on some of these routes.

Military Roads

In 1724 General Wade was sent to Scotland by King George I to report on the state of the Highlands and make recommendations for ensuring peace among the clans. One of Wade's proposals was to improve communications by making proper roads between the various garrisons which had been established some years earlier at Inverness, Fort William and Kilcumein (Fort Augustus), and in 1724 he began making proper roads to replace the old rough tracks, work which explains the old lines:

> *If you'd seen these roads before they were made,*
> *You'd lift up your hands and bless General Wade.*

By 1734 Wade's soldiers had made some 250 miles of roads:
1. Fort William to Fort Augustus and by Whitebridge to Inverness.
2. Dunkeld to Inverness by the Drumochter Pass.
3. Crieff to Dalnacardoch.
4. Dalwhinnie to Fort Augustus by the Corrieyairack Pass.
5. Ruthven Barracks (Kingussie) to the Corrieyairack road.

His last work was the erection of the bridge over the River Tay at Aberfeldy, which bears an inscription that it was built in 1733, the first stone being put in place by Wade himself on 26th April. General Wade left Scotland in 1740; he died in 1748, with the rank of Field Marshal, and was buried in Westminster Abbey.

The road work in Scotland was carried on by Wade's successor, Major Caulfield, who had the title of Inspector of Roads, and was responsible for the construction between 1740 and 1767 of some 830 miles of military roads. These included:

1. Stirling to Crieff.
2. Dumbarton to Inveraray and Tyndrum by the Rest and be Thankful.
3. Stirling to Glen Coe and Fort William.
4. Coupar Angus to Fort George by Braemar, Tomintoul and Grantown.
5. Fettercairn by the Cairn o' Mount to Huntly and Fochabers.
6. Bridge of Sark (Gretna) to Portpatrick.
7. Fort Augustus to Bernera Barracks (Glenelg).
8. Aberdeen to Huntly.
9. Stonehaven to Aberdeen, Portsoy and Fochabers.
10. Stirling to Dumbarton.
11. Contin (Ross-shire) to Poolewe.

Some of these roads were in time abandoned, others were transferred in the 19th century to the county authorities for maintenance.

Modern Roads

Roads, as distinct from tracks, had their beginning in Scotland in 1617, when the Scottish Parliament made the justices of the peace responsible for "mending all highways". The old tracks were in bad condition through increasing traffic, and were quite unfit for coaches, introduced to Scotland in the early 17th century. Travellers commonly described these tracks as infamous, infernal, execrable, with deep pools and ruts of liquid mud, or with rocky channels worse than the bed of a river.

The statute of 1617 had little effect. A new Act in 1669 introduced the scheme of statute labour, whereby every man in the parish between the ages of 15 and 70 had to give six day's labour on the roads every year, and the highways were to be made 20 feet broad and fit for horses and carts in winter as well as in summer. There was a general reluctance to work, and the scheme was never a success.

From 1713 onwards it was gradually superseded by the turnpike system, under which the people using the roads paid tolls and the road trustees employed a staff of roadmen. The turnpike system was abolished in 1878, when the maintenance of roads was made the responsibility of the local authorities.

For historical reference the most useful early maps of Scotland showing roads are the following:

1654 Blaeu's Atlas. The first map showing roads, but only some in the Lothians, Renfrew and Berwickshire.
1679 Rob. Greene. Scotland, with main roads. 13 miles to one inch.
1745 Hermann Moll's Atlas. With main roads. Scales from 4 to 7 miles to 1 inch.
1746 T. Willdey. Map, showing Wade roads. 5 miles to 1 inch.
1755 Roy's Military Survey. The first really detailed map with roads. In the British Museum, never published.

Various county maps are mentioned in route descriptions. A complete list of maps is given in *The Early Maps of Scotland*, published by the Royal Scottish Geographical Society.

Rights of Way
    As stated above, many of the routes described in this book are rights of way, but there are many which are not. The inclusion of a route in this book does not, therefore, imply that it is a right of way.
    A right of way may be described as a route from one public place to another which has been used by the public for a specified period, known as the prescriptive period. The essential requirements for the creation of a right of way under the common law are these:

1. The track must run from one public place to another public place.
2. The track must follow a more or less defined route.
3. The track must have been used openly and peacably by members of the public otherwise than with the permission, express or implied, of the landowner.
4. It must have been so used without substantial and effective interruption for a period of 20 years or more.

A public place is a place to which the public may legitimately go; it may mean a public road, a market place, a town or village, a church or a churchyard. The extent of a right of way depends on the extent of its use in the past, and a right of way for pedestrians is not necessarily a right of way for vehicles, and a 'Private Road' notice on a right of way means that it is a private road as far as vehicles are concerned, but is still a right of way for pedestrians. The proprietor of the land is entitled to erect gates and fences across rights of way provided that they do not obstruct public passage. Where fences are erected, gates wide enough for pedestrians must be provided, and such gates must not be locked.

It an offence for a proprietor or anyone else to create an obstruction across a right of way, and the local authority has the power to remove any such obstruction and re-instate the route.

Much more could be written about the law relating to rights of way in Scotland, but that is rather outwith the scope of this book. Those wishing to learn more should read *Rights of Way: A Guide to the Law in Scotland* published by the Scottish Rights of Way Society.

NOTES

Equipment

It is assumed that the walker setting out on the exploration of hill tracks in Scotland is aware of the need for appropriate equipment and clothing. The routes described in this book vary from short low-level walks on dry, well made footpaths where strong boots and special clothing are not required, to long, rough and often trackless routes over high ground which is frequently wet and boggy, particularly in the west. In the latter case strong waterproof shoes or boots are needed, unless one is prepared to get wet feet, and suitable protective clothing, waterproof and windproof, should also be regarded as necessary.

It is also assumed that those who read this book and set out on the walks described in it will carry a map and compass, and be able to use them. Not all the routes described are visible on the ground as paths or tracks, and where there is no visible sign of a route the walker will have to find his own way, and if the visibility is bad may have to use a map and compass for navigation.

Tracks, Times and Distances

Many of the upland areas of Scotland are now crossed by tracks made for shooting and estate management purposes. Some of these are old tracks made many years ago which are now blending with the landscape, others are recently bulldozed tracks which have created very obvious scars over hills and moors, and others are the tracks of all-terrain vehicles which have been more recently introduced, and which when used over soft grassy ground tend to leave dark muddy tracks. There are also many rough roads that have been driven into the hills as part of forestry operations.

Some of these tracks and roads are on the lines of existing paths, others are not. Their existence is sometimes helpful to walkers, but frequently they do not go in the direction that the walker wants. The Ordnance Survey maps, even the most recent Landranger series, do not show all these tracks accurately, so the walker must be careful when map-reading to be aware of possible discrepancies.

The time required for any walk will depend on the the distance, the weather, the state of the path and the amount of uphill climbing involved. In the west and north-west of Scotland more than in the east, routes are likely to be over rough ground, paths may be faint or non-existent and the ground wet and boggy. All these factors make for slower progress than on good paths, and the normal walking rate of 3 miles per hour (4½km/h) is likely to be reduced to about 2 miles per hour (3km/h).

Another important factor to be considered in bad weather is the state of streams that may have to be crossed. If a stream is in spate and there is no bridge, then the crossing may be very difficult, dangerous or even impossible, and a long detour may be required to find an alternative crossing. It may even be necessary to turn back. These remarks apply particularly to the north-west Highlands where high rainfall and swollen streams are not uncommon. Take note of weather signs and forecasts before setting out.

Some of the walks described in this book go over mountainous country and reach heights up to 1000m. In winter these walks become full-scale mountain days, and those setting out on them must be adequately experienced and equipped for winter hillwalking (see page 14).

Transport and Accommodation

It is not the function of this book to provide detailed information and timetables for bus, train and ferry services in Scotland. This information is available from the offices of the various operating companies.

The very useful booklet *Getting Around the Highlands and Islands* that was published by the Highlands and Islands Development Board (latterly Highlands and Islands Enterprise) is unfortunately no longer produced. The last edition was published about 1991. Anyone with a recent copy of this booklet would be well advised to keep it, as much of the information in it is still of considerable use.

In many rural parts of Scotland, Royal Mail operate postbuses which, in addition to delivering mail, have seats for a few passengers. These services can be very useful to walkers in remote rural areas where there are no buses. Details of postbus services are published in the *Scottish Postbus Timetable*, published in several booklets for different parts of Scotland including the Borders, Dumfries & Galloway and the Highlands. These timetables are obtainable from Royal Mail Customer Service Centre, 1 George Square, Glasgow G2 1AA.

Information about accommodation in Scotland of all types – hotels, guest houses, bed and breakfast, and self catering – is published by the Scottish Tourist Board, 23 Ravelston Terrace, Edinburgh EH4 3EU in its books *Where to Stay in Scotland*. These books are available in many bookshops and tourist information offices.

There are many youth hostels in Scotland which are well placed for the walks described in this book. Information about hostels and membership of the Scottish Youth Hostels Association can be obtained from the National Office of the Association, 7 Glebe Crescent, Stirling FK8 2JA. There are also offices in Aberdeen, Ayr, Dundee, Edinburgh and Glasgow.

In some of the remote parts of the Borders, Galloway and the Highlands there are bothies which give shelter for walkers. Some of them are mentioned in this book. These bothies are small unlocked cottages with no furnishings or equipment, but they do provide simple overnight shelter for a few people. Many of them are maintained by the Mountain Bothies Association. Details about the Association's activities can be obtained from its Information Officer, Ted Butcher, 26 Rycroft Avenue, Peterborough PE6 8NT.

Maps

The most suitable maps for walkers are the Ordnance Survey 1:50,000 maps which have in the last twenty years superseded the One Inch to the Mile maps of earlier years. The latter are, however, still in use by many people. The other important maps for walkers are the Bartholomews Half Inch maps, and their successors the Bartholomews 1:100,000 maps. These are no longer in publication, but no doubt many walkers still use them.

In revising this book, the compilers have made use of the latest editions of the OS Landranger Series, which are the most recent versions of the 1:50,000 scale maps. As far as possible place names, spellings and heights used in this book correspond with those in the latest Landranger maps, whose revision dates are about 1988. Users of this book are recommended to use these maps also, as they are more accurate than earlier ones in depicting such features as woodland and forests, tracks and paths. However, not even the most recent maps are entirely accurate in showing paths, some of which have long since disappeared yet still appear on maps.

In each route description in this book, the relevant maps are listed thus: The OS 1:50,000 map number(s) before /, the One Inch to the Mile map number(s) after /, followed by the map number at the end of this book in bold.

Six-figure map references are given in the conventional way, the first three figures being the easting and the last three figures being the northing.

In the text the abbreviation m is used for metres height or vertical interval, while distances are quoted in metres and km (kilometres). Miles (mls) are only used for giving route lengths.

Gaelic Place Names

The following Gaelic words occur frequently in place names, and a knowledge of their meanings helps our understanding of the maps:

a', an	*the*	eas	*waterfall*
abhainn, amhainn	*river*	garbh	*rough*
allt	*burn, stream*	geal	*white*
aonach	*ridge*	glas, ghlas	*grey or green*
ban, bhan	*white*	gleann	*glen, valley*
beag, beg, bheag	*small*	gorm	*blue*
bealach	*pass*	lairig	*pass*
ben, beinn, bheinn		laogh, laoigh	*calf*
	hill, mountain	liath	*grey*
bidean, bidein	*peak*	lochan	*small loch*
braigh	*brae, hill-top*	meall	*rounded hill*
breac, bhreac	*speckled*	mor, mhor	*big*
buidhe, bhuidhe	*yellow*	na, nam, nan	*the, of,*
carn	*cairn, hill, pile of stones*		*of the*
clach	*stone, stony*	odhar	*dun-coloured*
coille	*wood*	ruadh	*red*
coire, choire	*corrie, hollow*	sgurr, stob, stuc	
creag	*crag, cliff, rock*		*peak (usually rocky)*
dearg	*red*	srath	*strath, wide valley*
drum, druim	*ridge*	uaine	*green*
dubh	*black, dark*		

THE COUNTRY CODE
published by the Countryside Commission for Scotland

Protect wildlife, plants and trees
Make no unnecessary noise
Take special care when driving on country roads
Use gates and stiles to cross fences, hedges and walls
Fasten all gates
Guard against all risk of fire
Keep to paths across farm land
Leave livestock, crops and machinery alone
Keep dogs under close control
Take your litter home
Help to keep all water clean
Respect the life of the countryside

In forests keep to the forest roads, tracks and rides (fire-breaks); do not light fires, avoid smoking and do not damage trees. The Forestry Commission encourages walkers to use forests for recreation, with the reservation that access may have to be restricted at times of high fire risk or for operational reasons such as felling.

Walkers and climbers should respect the legitimate rights and privacy of those who live and work in the countryside. When walking through farms, cultivated land and estate policies, follow paths or tracks, and where rights of way are known or signposted, they should be used. Particular care should be excercised when going through grazing land during the lambing season.

Restraint should be shown during the stalking and grouse-shooting seasons to avoid interfering with these activities, which are usually important economically for country estates. The dates of these activities are typically from 12th August to the end of October, but hind culling may continue until February. The public are entitled to walk along rights of way at all times, but consideration should be shown in the excercise of this right at sensitive times of the year.

The Mountaineering Council of Scotland and the Scottish Landowners Federation have jointly published a useful booklet *Heading for the Scottish Hills* which lists many estates in the Highlands and gives the addresses and telephone numbers of owners, factors and keepers who can be contacted for information about stalking and shooting activities. The use of this booklet is recommended to those who plan to walk across the hills and moors during the stalking and shooting seasons.

Mountain Safety
Bearing in mind that many of the walks described in this book take one over high ground, in some cases to mountain tops, and that in winter the conditions can be very severe, an appreciation of mountain safety is important. The following points should be kept in mind, particularly if you are planning a long, high route in winter:

Before you go:
Learn how to use a map and compass
Know the weather signs and forecast
Plan a route within your capability
Know simple first aid and be able to recognise the signs of
    exposure
Know the mountain distress signals

When you go:
Do not go alone
Leave information about your route
Take adequate spare clothing
Take map, compass, torch and food
Wear climbing boots
In winter take an ice axe
Recognise dangerous snow or ice slopes

As changes are always taking place in the countryside with new forest plantations and new tracks, some of the information given in this book will become out of date. The compilers would be glad to receive corrections in respect of any of the routes described in this book.
Please send any such information to:

**Scottish Rights of Way Society
10/2 Sunnyside, Edinburgh EH7 5RA**

A Brief History of the Scottish Rights of Way Society

By Douglas Lowe

Early Days; the First Period 1845 – 1882

Formed in 1845 as The Association for the Protection of Public Rights of Roadway in and around Edinburgh, it was soon active and dealing with disputed paths around the capital, Roslin Glen and Corstorphine Hill being prominent. Perhaps because of the cosmopolitan nature of the citizens of Edinburgh, the organisation began to look further afield, dealing with such diverse problems as access to the Field of Bannockburn and combating the attempts of early Victorian sporting estate owners to close many of the glens and hills to the walking public. It quickly evolved into a national organisation, and changed its name to The Association for the Protection of Public Rights of Roadway in Scotland.

The Association funded and organised the successful court action against the Duke of Atholl's attempts to close Glen Tilt to the walking public. This court case in 1847 was widely reported and did much to increase awareness of public rights of way in Scotland. Despite being hampered by lack of funds following the Glen Tilt case, the Association continued its work during the 1860s, after which it appeared to become rather inactive.

The Second Period, 1883 – 1922

In 1883 the Association was stung into action by an attempt to close one of the paths on its own doorstep in the Pentland Hills. It was reconstituted as The Scottish Rights of Way and Recreation Society Limited, and moved into arguably its most productive and influential period.

The Pentland paths were investigated and the first signposts were erected. The first guidebook to the Pentland paths was produced in 1885, and the first Bartholomew's map of the Pentland Hills appeared in 1890, John Bartholomew being one of the directors of the Society. Problems were reported from the North, and a small delegation, led by Walter A. Smith, set off in 1885 on an expedition to erect signs on many of the Grampian paths, including the Lairig Ghru, the Lairig an Laoigh and glens Feshie, Tromie, Tilt and Doll.

The action in the last named glen led directly to the celebrated Glen Doll court case in 1887 from which the Society emerged victorious, having successfully defeated an attempt to close the Glen Doll to Braemar route. Duncan Macpherson of Glen Doll had contested the action vigorously from the Courts of Session up to the House of Lords and, having lost, had to bear costs of £5000, a substantial sum in those days. For a long period after this case there was a reluctance on the part of landowners to contest the rights of walkers to travel along these ancient routes. The costs of the Glen Doll case to the Society were £650-7-4d, a sum which came close to bankrupting it.

The substantial costs arising from the Glen Doll court case led directly to the Society's sponsoring of a Right of Way Bill through Parliament which saw important additions being made to the Local Government Scotland Act 1894 where, for the first time, direct responsibility for rights of way matters was imposed on local authorities. The Society's board, which at that time included three MPs, James Bryce, T.R.Buchanan and Peter Esslemont, felt that the Act was satisfactory but would not be complete until a simpler and cheaper method for this legal process had been found.

The Society had also supported James Bryce's Access to Mountains (Scotland) Bills, (1884,1888 and 1892). Continuing their high profile, brought by the success and publicity of the Glen Doll case, the Society kept a watching brief of the various Railway Bills that were going through Parliament, seeking to preserve any rights of way that might be threatened by new railway lines. It was a very busy time for the Society: investigating, negotiating, erecting signposts where possible, and declaring in 1891 that they were "dealing with disputes in 17 of the 32 counties of Scotland."

The influence of the 1894 Local Government Act, whereby Local Authorities in the form of the Parish Councils took responsibility for rights of way, began to be felt and in the years 1904 to 1923 the Society's activities partially lapsed as its work overlapped with the Parish Councils. Indeed, the Society was warned on a few occasions not to interfere. It continued intermittently to deal with matters such as the Lochaber Water Supply Bill, where as a result of raising the level of some lochs for hydro-electric power purposes, paths would be submerged and lost.

Modern Times, 1923 to 1945

In the years following the 1894 Act the need for the Society should have diminished, but by the early 1920s it was apparent that the Local Authorities were not exercising their powers adequately. The Society re-emerged in 1923, doing much signposting work in the Pentland Hills and throughout the country, recognising that signposting was important both in publicising and preserving rights of way paths.

From early days the Society had been assembling information and evidence on rights of way routes, indeed in 1891 one of the directors, John Blair, had suggested collecting evidence of routes from drovers and shepherds who in those days were still in the habit of taking their beasts to market on foot. The year 1924 saw the publication of Walter Smith's book *Hill Paths in Scotland*, which was a distillation of much of the Society's work. Smith had been on the Board since 1883 and was Chairman from 1904 to 1931.

The Society became involved in the dispute at Glen Tanar on Deeside, and also kept a watch over the growing number of hydro-electric schemes. It managed also to preserve for the walking public part of the Old Glencoe Road across the Black Mount, which continues to be heavily used today as it forms part of the West Highland Way long distance path.

1946 until the present

At the start of the Second World War the Society's signs, together with all other road signs, had been removed so that any invading army's progress might be hampered (and their recreational opportunities restricted). The Society was reconstituted as the Scottish Rights of Way Society Limited in 1946 and began systematically to re-erect the signs which had been removed. Disputes still arose, but modern times also brought more modern problems. More hydro-electric schemes threatened to submerge and extinguish ancient paths; plans for large-scale road schemes and motorways had to be examined and the Society's role as public watchdog continued. Much work was done in liaising with Local

Authorities on rights of way matters and, following the 1967 Countryside (Scotland) Act, in trying to get Local Authorities to list and record rights of way in their areas.

In recent years concern has been expressed at the loss of rights of way and other paths as a result of the rapid development of forestry in Scotland. Negotiation between the Society and the Forestry Commission a few years ago led to an Accord between the two parties which it is hoped will arrest the loss of rights of way as a result of forest planting.

Following the 1984 Act the Board had expressed satisfaction, but said that matters could not be considered to be complete until a simpler and cheaper method for resolving rights of way disputes was found. In 1990 the Society, with the guidance of its then Chairman Professor A.E.Anton, submitted to the Secretary of State for Scotland a proposal for the reform of the law relating to rights of way which, if enacted, would bring about this hundred-year-old wish.

The recently published report from Scottish Natural Heritage *Enjoying the Outdoors* has restated the need for a reform of the law, and the prospect now exists that something will be done to replace the time-consuming and expensive legal processes that presently exist by a simpler and less expensive administrative system. Such a change would be helpful to Local Authorities in carrying out their responsibilities, and would benefit the public.

At the formation of the original Association in 1845, Adam Black, co-founder of A & C Black, Publishers, and who was then the Lord Provost of Edinburgh, delivered the founding motion: "That it would prove highly beneficial to the inhabitants of towns, many of whom were employed in sedentary occupations and pent up in crowded houses in narrow streets and closes, were they to enjoy such facilities for taking recreation in the country as might tend to promote their health of body and vigour of mind." Archaic language, but carrying an important social message which is equally true today.

Adam Black's words and actions were surprisingly forward-thinking for mid-19th century Edinburgh, but his forward thinking was imbued into the ethos of the Society, and much of the quiet, efficient work over the last 150 years has had a long-term effect that was not fully appreciated at the time.

The Society has gone to the courts where necessary, when all else has failed, but as mentioned much of its work over the past century and a half has been quiet and efficient. By negotiation and agreement, by judicious signposting, and by taking a stand where necessary, Scotland's great heritage of rights of way has been preserved and increased. Drove roads, old military roads, kirk roads, coffin roads; many of these trails that we now follow owe their continued existence to the Society's vigilance. All of us who walk, hike or ramble among Scotland's hills and glens owe a debt to the Society, a debt that can be recognised through membership of the Society and support of its essential and continuing work.

SECTION 1
The Cheviot Hills

Across the Cheviots run some of the oldest tracks in Scotland. The earliest that can be dated is the Roman road Dere Street, constructed and used by the Romans between AD 78 and 185. In 1296 Edward I travelled along the Wheel Causeway. The Redeswire crossing, now the Carter Bar road, is mentioned in 1375 in Barbour's *Brus*. A state paper of 1543 (*Henry VIII Domestic Series XVIII, part 2, No. 538*), gives the following seventeen crossings of the Cheviots:

1. White Swire (White Law) (route 1).
2. Pete Swire.
3. Cribhead, Smalden Road and Roughside – crossing Auchope Rig between Auchope Cairn and The Schil. Another list of 1597 refers to one crossing as Auchope Swire.
4. Hunt Road, apparently over Butt Roads (524m), 5km SW of The Cheviot.
5. Hexpethgate (route 3).
6. Maiden Cross (route 5).
7. Black Braes (route 6).
8. Hindmoor Well (over Lamb Hill).
9. Hewghen Gate (over Rushy Fell).
10. Gamel's Path (route 7).
11. Phillip's Cross (omitted in 1543, but included in a list of 1547) (route 8a).
12. Almond Road (route 8b).
13. Redeswire (Carter Bar road).
14. Carter – Carter Fell is 5km W of Carter Bar (a track crosses Knox Knowe on the W of Carter Fell – see route 9).
15. The Wheel Causeway (route 10).
16. Bells – the road by Deadwater.
17. Kershopehead – E of Newcastleton.

1 Kirk Yetholm to Kirknewton
13km/8mls   *Maps: OS 74/70,71; 1*

Go E by road to the Halter Burn, cross this and go over the S shoulder of Green Humbleton, then SE between Madam Law and White Law to Trowupburn, down to the College Burn, thence N down the valley by Hethpool to Kirknewton. From Green Humbleton a shorter and more northerly track goes over to the Elsdon Burn; or from Trowupburn a farm road goes N to the Elsdon Burn and down to Hethpool.

2 Kirk Yetholm to Wooler by The Cheviot
29km/18mls   *Maps: OS 74,75/70,71; 1*

Follow the Halter Burn up to Burnhead, then go SE up the slope of Latchly Hill to the col between The Curr and Black Hag, then SE to the Border. Follow the Border ridge S over The Schil (601m) and round the head of the College Burn to Auchope Cairn and The Cheviot (815m).

This is all part of the Pennine Way. From The Cheviot go due E down its slope to Langleeford Hope and down the Harthope Burn to Wooler.

The walk can be shortened by omitting The Cheviot. From the S shoulder of Black Hag descend E by the Fleehope Burn to Fleehope and Southernknowe, then turn SE up the Lambden Burn to Goldscleugh. From there continue up the burn for 1km and then turn N between Preston Hill and Broadhope Hill to Broadstruther, from where a farm road goes E over Steely Crag to the Harthope Burn road.

An alternative from Southernknowe is to go steeply uphill due E, then NE over the moor to Commonburn House, from where a farm road goes E to Wooler.

3 Kirk Yetholm to Alwinton
31km/19mls   *Maps: OS 74,80/70,71; 1*

From Town Yetholm go S by the B6401 road to Primsidemill, then SE by Clifton up Kaim Rig and the E shoulder of Black Hill and through forest to the col between The Curr and Blackdean Curr, then down to Auchope and Schilgreen in the Sourhope valley. From

Schilgreen go S over the hill to the Dod Burn and S over the hill to Cocklawfoot. (This point may also be reached from Primsidemill by road up the Bowmont Water).

From Cocklawfoot go SE up Cock Law to the Border west of Butt Roads (524m), and S by Hazely Law, across the Usway Burn and by Clennell Street past Nettlehope Hill and Wholehope Knowe to Alwinton in Coquetdale. From Hazely Law there are alternative routes by the Usway Burn or by Barrow Law and Barrow Burn down the River Coquet.

This old crossing of the Border was known as Hexpethgate; the Cocklaw was a regular meeting place for the Wardens of the Marches. On Roy's map of 1755 this route is shown as a road, and marked 'Road from Morpeth to Kelso'. South of the Border the track has the name of Clennell Street.

4 Kirk Yetholm to Byrness by the Pennine Way
43½km/27mls   *Maps: OS 74,80/70; 1*
The Pennine Way goes E from Kirk Yetholm across the Halter Burn and up over the S shoulder of Green Humbleton to the ridge which forms the line of the Border. Then it follows the Border over White Law, Black Hag (549m) and The Schil (601m) to Auchope Cairn (726m). The Pennine Way diverges here to take in The Cheviot (815m) and returns to follow the Border ridge SW to Dere Street and the Roman camps at Chew Green. In another 1½km the Pennine Way turns S over Ravens Knowe and Windy Crag to Byrness on the A68 road.

5 Kirk Yetholm to Byrness
30½km/19mls   *Maps: OS 74,80/70; 1*
From Kirk Yetholm go by road up the Bowmont Water to Mowhaugh, then SW up the Hall Burn, across The Street between Windy Law and Craik Moor, and down to Greenhill on the Heatherhope Burn. Continue SW up the Capehope Burn to Buchtrig and by the E of Haughigshaw Hill to join Dere Street, 1km E of Towford. Finally go SE by Dere Street to the Roman camps at Chew Green (route 7), and then W and S by the Pennine Way (route 4) to Byrness.

6 Morebattle to Alwinton by The Street
32km/20mls   *Maps: OS 74,80/70,71; 1*

From Morebattle (7km SW of Town Yetholm) a road goes S up the Kale Water to Hownam (7km). From there go E uphill by a track called The Street, which runs SE over Windy Law, Craik Moor and Green Knowe (415m) to the Border. (This point may also be reached from Town Yetholm by road up the Bowmont Water to Mowhaugh, thence S by the Calroust Burn to join The Street less than ½km N of the Border).

The fact that 7km of the parish boundary between Hownam and Morebattle runs along The Street shows that it is a very old highway. On Roy's map of 1755 this track across the Border is named 'Clattering Path'.

From the Border, The Street goes S over Black Braes and along a ridge to Hindside Knowe, then it drops down to the road in Coquetdale 1km NW of Barrow Burn and 10km from Alwinton.

It should be noted that on the English side of the Border there is an extensive artillery range and danger area (marked on the OS maps), which restricts the use of some alternative routes.

7 Jedburgh to Rochester by Dere Street
35km/21mls   *Maps: OS 74,80/70; 1*

This is a splendid route for walkers over the Cheviots as Dere Street is mostly a broad grassy track. From the bridge at Jedfoot, where the A698 crosses the Jed Water 3km N of Jedburgh, it runs straight for 8km *via* Cappuck (Roman fort) to Shibden Hill, thence by Whitton Edge, Pennymuir (camp), over the Kale Water at Tow Ford, and SE by Blackhall Hill to the Border at Black Halls. It then goes S for 1km to the extensive Roman camps at Chew Green, thence SE by Outer Golden Pot (now as a road) to Featherwood, and then down a straight 5km S to Bremenium (camps) and Rochester, from where it is a further 8km by road to Otterburn.

The Roman Road can be reached at Tow Ford by road from Hownam. From Chew Green southward the road lies within an artillery range, and for that reason starting from Rochester is advisable as enquiry about the firing can be made at Redesdale Camp.

From the Jed Water, Dere Street ran N to the Eildon Hills. Although partly overgrown, 6km of it can still be followed from the B6400 road on the N side of the River Tweed at 647250 NW to Forest Lodge on the A68. This was the main Roman road into Scotland, in use by the Romans between AD 78 and 185. It ran from Durham to the Forth and has been traced to Dalkeith. In the Middle Ages this road, where it crossed the Cheviots, was known as Gamel's Path.

8 Edgerston to Byrness
16km/10mls   *Maps: OS 80/70;* **1**

The route described in a previous edition of this book from Edgerston to Byrness *via* Ephope Law is now impracticable due to afforestation; the Leithope Forest ride south is also very difficult. An alternative is possible, starting from the Wooplaw road end at 690089 on the A68 near Edgerston 14½km S of Jedburgh by road (bus). By a forest road go *via* Arks to Fawhope, continue by the track along the N edge of Leithope Forest and at its NE corner turn S to cottages near Upper Hindhope. From there go SE over Whiteside Hill to join the Pennine Way at 773083 near Coquet Head, thence S over Windy Crag (490m) to Byrness.

9 Edgerston to Kielder
22½km/14mls   *Maps: OS 79,80/70;* **1**

(a) From Edgerston go SW by road over Hareshaw Knowe to the Hawick Road (A6088), then S from Carterhouse Farm by an old road to the quarry and then a forestry road which ascends to the Border at Carter Fell and continues S to Limestone Knowe (549m). From there go by the march fence to Grey Mare's Knowe, then descend due S to Kielder Head and SW by a forest road down the Kielder Burn to Kielder Village. In 1543 this was known as the Carter Route as the track crosses Carter Fell. (Afforestation is proceeding and may affect this route).

(b) Alternative: On joining the Hawick road, turn right for 1km and go SW beside a plantation, across the Carter Burn and up a track through the forest to a point about 100 metres before the bridge at Burns Cottage. There the track turns off left on the E of the Black

Burn and climbs uphill to Knox Knowe (499m), cairn on the Border. Descend SE to the Garry Burn, then go up the slope of Grey Mare's Knowe, keeping to the high ground, and from the top descend as in (a).

10 Bonchester Bridge to Sauchtree or Kielder by the Wheel Causeway
24km/15mls   *Maps: OS 80/70; 1*

From Bonchester Bridge go S along the road by Braidhaugh to Cleuch Head, where a track climbs SE to the E side of Wolfelee Hill and goes S over Wardmoor Hill. The Wheel Causeway enters Wauchope Forest where the trees form a right-angled corner. From there take the middle of three rides which start from the corner and follow this wider than usual ride S for 6km through the forest to a gate a little to the W of Wheelrig Head (447m). It can become overgrown, but is cleared periodically by the Forestry Commission.

From the gate go SSW for 400 metres and follow a forest road down the E side of Wormscleuch Burn to Myredykes. (To follow the actual line of the Wheel Causeway S of Wheelrig Head is now very difficult). From Myredykes it is 6km S to Kielder.

In mediaeval times the Wheel Causeway was the road from Roxburgh, then the largest town in the Borders, to Annandale. Edward I travelled along this route in 1296. On Roy's map it is named 'Road to Jedburgh'. It is marked as a road on Stobie's 1770 map of Roxburghshire as running from Easter Fodderlee by the E side of Abbotrule and Doorpool to Spar.

11 Newcastleton to Kielder
27km/17mls   *Maps: OS 79,80/76; 1*

Follow the road up the Liddel Water for 7km to Dinlabyre, then go SE uphill by a forestry road to Larriston Fells. (Take the right-hand fork at 550909). Continue by the track to Bloody Bush on the Border, then down by the Grains Burn and Akenshaw Burn to The Forks, and down the Lewis Burn to Lewisburn, from where it is 4km N by road to Kielder. This is an old road used in the early 19th century for the transport of coal from Northumberland. Bridges on the road have the date 1828. On the Border there is a monument giving distances along the road.

Dere Street to Whitton Edge across the Cheviots (route 7)

Looking up Glen Sax towards Dun Rig (route 22)

Green Cleuch in the Pentland Hills (route 48)

On the Enterkin Pass, looking south (route 63)

Alternatively, just past Akenshawburn, cross a stone bridge and turn left up a forest road for 450 metres. At the point where this road bends right, go straight on uphill and descend NW. The path, 5km long, is marked by yellow discs (see Border Forest Guide).

SECTION 2
The Border Country

12 Hawick to Newcastleton by the Thieves' Road
32km/20mls   *Maps: OS 79/69;* **1**

Go S by the road *via* Pilmuir and Dodburn to Dod, then due S uphill and along the ridge by the Thieves' Road over Dod Rig to Swire Knowe (459m), and down by Braidleyhope to the Hermitage Water. It is then 12km by road to Newcastleton. The alternative is to go uphill S from Dinley, then by Thief Sike and Hartsgarth to Redheugh, 3km from Newcastleton.

Starting from Roberton, go SE over the hill by Parkhill and the N side of Branxholme Easter Loch to Newmill, then still SE up Allan Water to join the Dodburn Road. Newmill is also reached by bus from Hawick.

An almost parallel route starts from the old Stobs Camp, 5½km S of Hawick on the B6399 road. From there go SW up the ridge by a broad track to White Hill, then S by Peelbraehope to Hawkhass. Follow the forest track SE to reach Scaw'd Law and from there go along Sundhope Rig to Sundhope and the Newcastleton road.

13 Roberton to Teviothead
11km/7mls   *Maps: OS 79/69;* **1**

Take the road up Borthwick Water to the bridge at Muselee, then go S uphill by a broad track to Broadlee Loch. Keep it on the left and continue S over High Seat and Dryden Fell, and descend by Dryden to the River Teviot and Teviothead (bus route).

14 Eskdalemuir to Roberton and Hawick by Craik Cross
37km/23mls   *Maps: OS 79/89;* **1,2**

In its first part this is an old Roman road, probably linking the Annandale Roman road with Dere Street (see route 7). Eskdalemuir is 21km by road (B709) up Eskdale from Langholm. Leave this road where it turns left to cross the Esk, and follow the road going N on the E side of the river over the hill to Raeburnfoot Farm. (Roman fort on the left). From there go up the Rae Burn for 2km, then uphill NE over Craik Muir and Lamblair Knowe to Craik Cross Hill (451m), the highest point on the route. This part of the route is through the extensive Eskdalemuir and Craik forests.

Beyond this point keep NE on the top of the ridge by the forest road going down to Craik. This road does not coincide throughout with the line of the Roman road. From Craik a road goes down Borthwick Water to Roberton. To reach Hawick leave this road at Muselee, where it crosses the stream, and go E uphill to join the secondary road which goes E by Branxholme Easter Loch to the Teviot valley. The walking distance may be shortened by going S from Craik to Old Howpasley and then E to Lairhope and Teviothead. (bus; see route 31).

R.P.Hardie in *The Roads of Mediaeval Lauderdale* suggests that this may also be the road referred to in a 13th-century charter as the royal road from the valley of the Annan towards Roxburgh.

15 Moffat to Eskdalemuir

22¹/₂km/14mls   *Maps: OS 78,79/69; 2*

From Moffat take the Wamphray road across the Moffat Water, then go left to Craigbeck, from where a forestry road goes up the Cornal Burn to its source. The forestry road turns S down Wamphray Water, and in about 400 metres a path leaves the road and goes steeply uphill and E over Cowan Fell. This path (faint) continues E and meets another forestry road on the col between Dun Moss and Loch Fell. This road leads down the Big Strushel Burn and Garvald Water to the B709 road at Garvaldwaterfoot, 3km N of Eskdalemuir. Part of this route coincides with the Southern Upland Way.

16 Moffat to Ettrick (Tushielaw)

30¹/₂km/19mls   *Maps: OS 78,79/69; 2*

(a) Follow route 15 to the Wamphray Water, then follow the path N to its source. At the watershed the path crosses to the Selcoth Burn above Craigmichan Scar and then goes NE to Ettrick Head, between Capel Fell and Wind Fell. From there it is downhill by Ettrick Water to Potburn, and thence by road to Tushielaw.

The walking distance can be shortened by starting from the A708 road 7km NE of Moffat at Shortwoodend. Cross the Moffat Water to Sailfoot Farm and Selcoth Farm, and follow the path on the S side of the Selcoth Burn to join the previous route

(b) An alternative is by road up Moffat Water to Capplegill (9km). At that point cross the Water to Bodesbeck and follow the track going E uphill on the N side of the Bodesbeck Burn, crossing the ridge and descending into the Ettrick Valley at Potburn.

This was the original road from Moffat to Selkirk. On Ainslie's 1772 map of Selkirkshire the mileages are given and the pass above Bodesbeck is named 'Peneracross Road'. Roy's map of 1755 names it 'Road to Hawick'.

17 Tweedsmuir to Moffat
26km/16mls   *Maps: OS 72,78/68,69; 2*

From Tweedsmuir cross the River Tweed and take the road to Fruid Reservoir, where there is good parking at the dam. Follow the road along the NE side of the reservoir. From Fruid Farm a rough road goes round the head of the reservoir. Continue past its end and towards Macrule Hill where a track can be seen slanting up its W slope. After about 1½km the track bends left and becomes indistinct. Keep uphill to round the W slope of Ballaman Hill where two cairns can be seen at 089163. From there two routes are possible:

(a) Go round Ballaman Hill and strike SSW (watch the direction very carefully) and cross the source of the Glencraigie Burn. Continue SSW, keeping E of Crown of Scotland, to cross Whitehope Burn and reach the col E of Chalk Rig Edge. From there go steeply down to the Annan valley at Ericstane, and finally go 6km by road from there to Moffat.

(b) From the W side of Ballaman Hill strike SW across Barncorse Knowe to Earlshaugh where a path goes S to the top of the Devil's Beef Tub. The path which continues down and across its W side can be dangerous. Instead, after crossing the old county boundary fence turn left and go along it for about 800 metres to turn S again and go down the incline of The Skirtle to Corehead and on to Ericstane and Moffat.

18 Broughton to St Mary's Loch
24km/15mls   *Maps: OS 72,73/69; 2*
   Leave Broughton by road to Drumelzier, then go SE up to Den
Knowes and by the Thief's Road over Den Knowes Head. Then go
by the W shoulder of Pikestone Hill, Long Grain Knowe, Dollar Law
(817m), Notman Law, Shielhope Head and Greenside Law, and
from there 900 metres E to join route 21 down to Glengaber and St
Mary's Loch. This is a very fine ridge walk over the 600m level.
   From Dollar Law one can return to Broughton by going S to Dun
Law then SW over Cramalt Craig to the radio beacon on Broad Law
from where a road descends to the River Tweed close to the Crook
Hotel, 11km S of Broughton.

19 Broughton to Peebles
19km/12mls   *Maps: OS 72,73/69; 2*
   From Broughton go up NE through Broughton Place farm and
keep straight on along the old drove road, which crosses Hollows
Burn and climbs to the col between Broomyside and Hammer
Head. On passing through the gate, keep E along the drove road,
rising slightly to cross the E shoulder of Hammer Head at approx
400m. Then drop down, cross the road to Stobo Hopehead and
cross the Hopehead Burn by a bridge below a conspicuous sheep
fank. Passing this, the drove road climbs SE to a col S of Midhill and
descends to Harrow Hope (ruin), whence follow the road on the N
side of Easton Burn to Stobo Kirk. Turn right along the public road
for 400 metres, then left across the River Tweed to Easter Dawyck
farm. Go up E to the col (400m) and down to The Glack. Cross the
Manor Water, turn S to Cademuir and then NE over Cademuir Hill
to Peebles.

20 Stobo to Yarrow
22½km/14mls   *Maps: OS 73/69, 2*
   From Stobo (11km SW of Peebles) at 175364 cross the River
Tweed and go SE over the hill by the Dead Wife's Grave, on the old
drove road between Hunt Law and Whitelaw Hill, to the Manor
Valley. Cross the Manor Water to Glenrath and go up the Glenrath
Burn by Glenrathhope and over Whitecleuch Hill to Drycleuch Law

and Muttonhall. Finally go down the Douglas Burn by Blackhouse to the Yarrow road (A708) 1½km from the Gordon Arms. (See also route 22).

21 Peebles to St Mary's Loch by the Manor Valley
27½km/17mls   *Maps: OS 73/69; 2*
    From the S end of the Tweed Bridge turn right and go along Caledonian Road, turn left at the end and go up Edderston Road to a gate with a 'Right of Way' sign, and over Cademuir Hill to the Manor Valley Road. Continue up the valley and 1km before Manorhead cross the Manor Water by a track and go S past Redsike Head, over the spur of Black Rig and down to Glengaber on the Megget Water, 2km W of St Mary's Loch.

22 Peebles to St Mary's Loch
21km/13mls   *Maps: OS 73/69; 2*
    For this fine ridge walk go SE from Peebles by Springhill Road and its continuation by path, and across the Haystoun Burn at Gipsy Glen to the wide old drove road which ascends the hill and runs for some distance along the ridge, over Kailzie Hill, Kirkhope Law and Birkscairn Hill. The route is then downhill to the E of Stake Law (keep to a height of about 500m round the head of the Quair Water glen) and Whiteknowe Head, then SSE down to the Douglas Burn and Blackhouse (where James Hogg, the Ettrick Shepherd, was herd from 1790 to 1800).
    It is 3km down the Douglas Burn to the Yarrow Road and another 1½km to the Gordon Arms. At Blackhouse the drove road joins route 23 and strikes SW over the hill to Dryhope at the foot of St Mary's Loch.
    For an alternative route from Peebles to Birkscairn Hill, go by Bonnington Road to Bonnington Farm, turn left past this farm to the Glensax Burn and go up this burn to Glensax. Then climb SE up the hillside to the ridge ½km S of Birkscairn Hill.
    This old drove road is the continuation of the drove road which led from Falkirk through the Cauldstane Slap in the Pentlands (route 51) and across the Meldon Hills (route 42). On Ainslie's map of Selkirkshire in 1772 it is marked 'Road to Peebles'.

23 Innerleithen to St Mary's Loch
23km/14mls   *Maps: OS 73/69; 2*

Cross the River Tweed to Traquair and from the church (at the cottage immediately S of the churchyard) go SW up the hill to Blake Muir, and by the E side of Deuchar Law to Blackhouse. There cross the Douglas Burn and go SW over by the W of Ward Law to Dryhope at the foot of St Mary's Loch. Cross the Yarrow Water and continue along the SE side of the loch to Tibbie Shiels Inn.

This route is part of the Southern Upland Way.

On Edgar's 1741 map of Peeblesshire this route is shown as the only road from the Tweed to the south. The original route from Edinburgh to the south is shown on Moll's map of 1725 as going by Dalhousie, near Temple, and over the Moorfoot Hills. It then went down the Leithen Water to Traquair. From the ford at the foot of St Mary's Loch the route continued by the Bridge Road over Altrieve Rig to Tushielaw, and on southwards. On Roy's map of 1755 the road is named 'Muir Road from Ettrick and Yarrow to Lothian Edge and Dalhousie'. A branch to Moffat went up the other side, ie the SE side of St Mary's Loch.

24 Traquair (Innerleithen) to Yarrow and Ettrick
14½km/9mls   *Maps: OS 73/69; 1*

Go SE from Traquair by Damhead Farm and up the ridge between the Fingland Burn and Curly Burn, over to Glengaber, then SE to the dip between Glengaber Hill and Peatshank Head, and down to Deuchar Tower and Yarrow (10km). Cross the Yarrow and go up the road to the top of Witchie Knowe, then down by the Tower Burn to Ettrickbridge.

25 Traquair to Yarrowford and Selkirk by Minchmoor
22½km/14mls   *Maps: OS 73/69; 1*

From Traquair Riggs go SE up the hill by the old road to the Cheese Well (490m) and over the N shoulder of Minch Moor (567m). Continue E over Hare Law, beyond which the route divides, the Minchmoor road bending to the right and going SE downhill to Yarrowford and Broadmeadows youth hostel, 13km from Innerleithen.

To reach Selkirk, keep due E after crossing Hare Law along the ridge and over Brown Knowe and Broomy Law. Keep to the S of the Three Brethren (cairns), and then turn downhill to the right and descend by the N side of Long Philip Burn to Philiphaugh Farm, close to Selkirk.

This old road between Traquair and Selkirk, now part of the Southern Upland Way, was in use in the 13th century as part of the road between Kelso Abbey and the Abbey lands at Lesmahagow. The original road kept to the N of Peat Law (it is marked on the map as 'Picts Work') and went down to a bridge which once crossed the Ettrick near Bridgelands (Lindean). Edward I travelled over the Minchmoor Road in 1296.

In 1305 the tenant of 'Westropkeliok' was bound to find a man at St James's Day for eight days during Roxburgh Fair to keep the road through Minche Moor from robbers *(Calendar Docs. relating to Scotland, Vol. 2, No. 1675)*. The later Minchmoor Road (as shown by Roy's map of 1755) is the one by Yarrowford. Dr John Brown describes it in his essay *Minchmoor:* "You go up the wild old Selkirk road which passes almost right over the summit, and by which Montrose and his cavaliers fled from Philiphaugh, where Sir Walter's mother remembered crossing, when a girl, in a coach and six, on her way to a ball at Peebles, several footmen marching on either side of the carriage to prop it up or drag it out of the moss hags...".

Another track branches to the right 1½km from Traquair, keeps to the right of Minch Moor (567m), and descends by the Lewenshope Burn to Yarrow, 2½km W of Yarrowford.

26 Galashiels to Yarrowford (Broadmeadows)
13km/8mls   Maps: OS 73/69; **1**

From the Mercat Cross go upwards past Galashiels Academy and (at 486354) follow Southern Upland Way guide posts SW over Hogg Hill to Yair Bridge. Turn right and go uphill behind Yair House SW for 3km until the Southern Upland Way turns NW on emerging from the forest N of Peat Law at 439312.

Leaving the Southern Upland Way there, the route goes W and after crossing the Long Phillip Burn ascends the N shoulder of

Foulshiels Hill, affording an exquisite panorama of the Yarrow valley before dropping to Broadmeadows youth hostel and Yarrowford.

An alternative is to start at the former Peel Hospital and go from its W side (signpost 'Williamthorpe') up the Glenkinnon Burn for 1½km, then S uphill to the E shoulder of Broomy Law. Make for the prominent cairn just above the 380m contour, from where it is a short descent to Broadmeadows.

27 Ettrickbridge to Roberton or Hawick
19km/12mls   *Maps: OS 73,79/69; 1*
There are three possibilities for this route:

(a) Cross the Ettrick and take the track going first SW and then S round Helmburn Hill until it meets another track on the left. Bear SE, passing between The Dod (364m) and Akermoor Loch to Langhope and Todrig. Continue S over Whitslaid Hill, and from Whitslaid go SE to Blawearie, from where roads lead to Roberton and Hawick. From Todrig a road goes by Easter Essenside to Ashkirk on the A7 (bus route).

(b) As in (a) for 600 metres, then keep SW uphill and over Shaw's Hill to Shaws, then S up by a wood to Shaws Mid Hill. From there go SE to the E side of Shaws Upper Loch, then turn SW to Gildiesgreen and along Hurkle Rig to the B711 road, 10km from Roberton.

(c) From Ettrickbridge take the Selkirk road for almost 2km and just before reaching Hutlerburn turn right up Hungry Hill, and go up to the N shoulder of Hutlerburn Hill. Then go SE to Essenside Loch and Easter Essenside. There cross the Ale Water to Burnfoot and in another 200 metres strike SE uphill and across the moor to Whitehaughmoor and Stintyknowes, 2½km by road from Hawick.

28 Yarrow to Ettrick or Roberton
13km/8mls or 27km/17mls   *Maps: OS 73,79/69; 1*
At Yarrow Feus (10km up the Yarrow from Broadmeadows) cross the Yarrow Water to Sundhope and go S between Sundhope Height and Scar Hill to Gilmanscleugh in the Ettrick valley. Cross the Ettrick Water to Easter Deloraine and go S up the Deloraine Burn to

Delorainehope. Continue due S up the Polloch Burn to the ridge, thence SE down to Deloraineshiel and the B711 road, 9km from Roberton.

Alternatively, from Delorainehope go SE up a burn to the col between Dun Knowe and Wedder Lairs and down SE to Drycleuchlee and the B711 road.

29 Gordon Arms to Tushielaw
8km/5mls   *Maps: OS 73,79/69; 2*

Go up the Ettrick road (B709) for 1½km, and about 160 metres beyond the Eldinhope Burn strike uphill on the left, climbing gradually S from the road to the col SW of Meg's Hill. Continue due S and after 2km go SE over Crookedside Hill and descend to Tushielaw.

30 Tibbie Shiels Inn to Tushielaw
11km/7mls or 18km/11mls   *Maps: OS 73/69; 2*

(a) From Tibbie Shiels Inn go E uphill (old road) to Earl's Hill, then S round Fall Law, E by the col (the 'Captain's Road') on the N of Cowan's Croft, and down the Hopehouse Burn to the B709 road, 1½km S of Tushielaw Inn.

(b) From Tibbie Shiels go S by the E side of the Loch of the Lowes, and then up the E side of the Riskinhope Burn and over Pikestone Rig to the col E of Peniestone Knowe. There a signpost indicates two routes: (1) down the W side of Scabcleuch Burn to the road at Scabcleuch, 1½km W of Ettrick, and (2) a more northerly route going SE along the flank of the hill and over to the path (formerly known as the Kirk Road) down by the Kirk Burn to the road at Ettrick Church (where James Hogg, the Ettrick Shepherd, is buried). Ettrick is 5km SW of Tushielaw Inn. This route follows part of the Southern Upland Way.

One of these routes is probably the Thirlestangate (gate = way) mentioned in a Melrose Charter of AD 1214-1249.

31 Tibbie Shiels to Hawick or Teviothead
31km/19mls   *Maps: OS 79/69; **1,2***

Follow route 30(b) to Ramseycleuch on the Ettrick and then go 3km S by road to Meerlees. From there go by a forest track (open to walkers) NE to Buccleuch. From East Buccleuch follow the estate road (old drove road) up to the forest at the SE corner of Kingside Loch, where the track meets a forest road. Go E for about 100 metres on this road, then turn off into the forest and follow a series of rides, maintaining an E course as far as possible. On emerging from the E side of the forest look for Girnwood Loch. The line of the old drove road passes about 300 metres N of the loch and goes by Hoscoteshiel (ruin) to Deanburnhaugh. (By following the burn flowing out of the loch S for 800 metres, another old drove road is met at 361118 also going E to Deanburnhaugh). From there go S by road for ½km to Muselee and continue E for 1½km to join and follow the the road S and E *via* Branxholme to Hawick.

To reach Teviothead two routes are possible:

(a) Go S uphill from Muselee by a broad track to Broadlee Loch, and continue S over High Street and Dryden Fell down to Dryden and Teviothead.

(b) From East Buccleuch go S by the farm road up the Rankle Burn for 4km to Baldhill. Continue S for 1km where a farm road comes in from the right; follow it S through the forest to Craik, where, on reaching the public road, turn right to its end opposite Howpasley. Continue up the Howpasley Burn and in 700 metres turn uphill on the left and go E by the S side of Rashy Hill and down by the Lairhope Burn to the River Teviot and Teviothead.

SECTION 3
The Lammermuirs and Moorfoots

32 Cockburnspath to Duns
27¹/₂km/17mls   *Maps: OS 67/63; 1*

From Cockburnspath go SW by road to Ecclaw Hill, and between it and Paits Hill leave the road to go S over the common to Bankend on the Monymut Water. Then go downstream for 1km to the bridge over the Whiteadder Water. In another 180 metres, opposite the church, turn right by the farm road up Abbey Hill and continue SW over the ridge reaching the Gifford to Duns road opposite Lodge Wood. Go up through this wood from a gate and continue S over the hill by Commonside and Black Hill (track only part of the way) to Harden's Hill, then another 5km by road to Duns. Part route of the Southern Upland Way.

33 Dunbar to Lauder (The Herring Road)
45km/28mls   *Maps: OS 67/63; 1*

Start by road to Spott and Spott Mill and S to Halls. Then go uphill to Dunbar Common, keeping to the W of Watch Law and then SSW over the upper reaches of Mossy Burn and West Burn, descending Sparleton Edge to the Whiteadder Water, 1km S of Johnscleugh. (If starting from Garvald instead of Dunbar, go 3km E to Stoneypath, then due S to Mid Hill and SE over Eachil Rig to Johnscleugh). Then go S to the Whiteadder Reservoir, round its N end to Penshiel and S to Kilpallet and Byrecleugh on Dye Water.

From Byrecleugh the alternatives are:

(a) E along the road to Dye Cottage and after crossing Dye Water go S by a good track to Wedderlie, then by road to Westruther or *via* Spottiswoode to Lauder;

(b) Up the Hall Burn and SW across the moor (no track) by Rutherford's Cairn to Gairnmuir or to Braidshawrig; from these cottages farm roads lead S to Blythe Farm 2½km by road from Dod Mill on the A697, and another 6½km from Lauder.

From Braidshawrig the direct and shortest route to Lauder is by an old track going SW across the moor on the W side of Blythe Water. When this track disappears at the Snawdon Burn, follow the field boundary ahead uphill to the summit. When the plantation ahead is in full view, make for the fence which leads to the S end of the wood. Go through the gate in this fence, and contouring the wood go through a second gate into the wood. There take the first turning left down to Wanton Walls Farm, about 3km by road from Lauder. Part of the Southern Upland Way.

An alternative route from Braidshawrig, not much longer and in some respects easier, is by the track NW over Edgarhope Law to the Earnscleugh Water, and down this valley to Newbigging Walls, 3km from Lauder.

The Herring Road was used in olden times by the country people bringing home a stock of salted herring for winter use. Only the first part between Dunbar and the Whiteadder is the original road; between Whiteadder and Lauder the Herring Road is shown on the old OS 6-inch map as going further north, over Hunt Law and Wedder Law. Roy's map of 1755 shows the road going over Meikle Says Law, Hunt Law and Wedder Law, and thence to Cleekhimin (2km S of Carfraemill) and Lauder, and calls it 'Muir Road from Lauder to Dunbar'.

34 East Linton to Cranshaws and Duns

22½km/14mls or 40km/25 mls   *Maps: OS 67/63; 1*

From East Linton take the road by Stenton and Ruchlaw West Mains to the foot of Deuchrie Dod, then ascend by Deuchrie to Dunbar Common. Keep straight on between the Mossy Burn and the West Burn to Beltondod and down the Bothwell Water to St Agnes and Cranshaws.

To reach Duns branch off left 500 metres S of St Agnes by a farm road up to Harehead Farm and continue uphill for another 500 metres to a broad grassy track running NW to SE. Go SE by this to Ellemford Bridge (4½km), and by road for another 1km to join route 32 at Lodge Wood.

35 Garvald to Longformacus
22½km/14mls   *Maps: OS 67/63; 1*

From Garvald go E to Stoneypath, reached also from Stenton or East Linton. Then go uphill, due S at first, to the highest point (398m) on Dunbar Common, and down S to Johnscleugh on the Whiteadder Water. Continue S by road to the reservoir, go round its northern end to Priestlaw Farm, and up over Priestlaw Hill to the Longformacus road. Cross this and go SE over Wether Law to Horseupcleugh, then down the N side of the Dye Water to Longformacus.

36 Cranshaws to Longformacus and Westruther
16km/10mls   *Maps: OS 67/63; 1*

(a) From the road 400 metres S of Cranshaws go uphill SW and then S by Redpath to Longformacus where there is a choice of routes:

(i) by road up the S bank of the Dye Water to Rawburn; in another 400 metres leave the road and continue SW across the moor to Wedderlie and the road to Westruther;

(ii) follow the Duns road for 800 metres, and at the top of the hill go SSW by the W side of Dirrington Great Law to Kippetlaw. Then strike SW for 3km (no path) to Evelaw, from where a road leads to Wedderlie and the road to Westruther. Part route of the Southern Upland Way.

(b) (Omitting Longformacus). From Cranshaws go up past the old church, and by a farm road and track round the S end of Long Wood and SE up over the moor (no path) to the Longformacus road. Cross this to the road leading to Horseupcleugh and Dye Cottage, from where a farm track goes S over the moor to Wedderlie (see route 36a).

37 Gifford to Carfraemill by Lammer Law
21km/13mls   *Maps: OS 66,67/63; 1*

From Gifford go S by Yester Mains to Long Yester, then SW by Blinkbonny Wood and up to the E shoulder of Lammer Law. Continue over Crib Law (509m) to Tollishill and by the Kelphope Burn down to Carfraemill Inn, 1½km from Oxton. This is a very old road, forming both a parish boundary and the old county boundary on the top of Lammer Law.

From Long Yester an alternative way is by the road to Hopes, West Hopes, and the S side of Hopes Reservoir, then up the Hopes Burn to join the above route on Crib Law.

38 Soutra Aisle to Melrose by the Girthgate

35½km/22mls   *Maps: OS 73/62,63,70; 1*

Soutra Aisle on Soutra Hill is reached by the A68 road to Soutra Mains and then by the B6368. Just beyond the Aisle an old grassy road is plainly visible as it goes S to cross the Armet Water. This was part of the Roman Dere Street, also in use in mediaeval times, and is well defined for 5km to the Roman camp at Kirktonhill (Channelkirk).

Beyond Kirktonhill the valley crossing is not now practicable and it is necessary to go left round to Oxton by road. The main street of Oxton leads directly uphill, and is continued by a track W of Overhowden to a point (477507) W of Collie Law; it is then necessary to go left uphill alongside a field dyke to the plantation on the ridge at 485501. (This can be more easily reached from Oxton by road *via* Bowerhouse).

The line of the old road is found on the W side of this plantation, and the ridge is followed S to Inchkeith Hill; watch the direction here after passing the farm buildings. This is the Girthgate; from Oxton the Roman Dere Street kept more to the E in the Leader Valley. The dyke along the ridge is the line until in sight of the Stow to Lauder road, at which point strike left to reach this road near its highest point. Then go left along the road until a cart track is seen on the right going S towards the E end of a wood. The track ends at a road junction SW of Threepwood. For a continuation to Melrose, in preference to the road down Allan Water, go 2½km E to join route 39 at Bluecairn.

This route is shown on Armstrong's 1773 map of the Lothians as starting from Soutra Aisle and going S to Threeburnford, and then by Collie Law as described above. It is named on that map and on the old OS 6-inch map as the 'Girthgate', i.e. sanctuary road, from some tradition that connected Soutra Hospice and Melrose Abbey.

As the road has been identified as the 'via regia' or royal road referred to in a Melrose Charter of 1180 (See R.P. Hardie, *The Roads of Mediaeval Lauderdale*), and Soutra was not founded until 1184, it seems that Soutra Hospice was founded because of the existing road. South of the Stow to Lauder road, the Girthgate formed the old county boundary for a mile.

39 Lauder to Melrose
16km/10mls   *Maps: OS 73/63,70;* **1**

Take the road up by the golf course, and 450 metres beyond Woodheads turn SSE alongside a plantation to Fordswell, and then go by road for 1km to Bluecairn. From there a fine broad track goes S over Kedslie Hill. Where it forks, take the left fork, pass Easter Housebyres, and go down to Gattonside and the footbridge to Melrose. This route follows part of the Southern Upland Way.

40 Leadburn to Heriot
27½km/17mls   *Maps: OS 73/62;* **1,2**

Take the Peebles road from Leadburn for just over 1km to Craigburn, then go NE on a track to Kingside. There turn SE following a track towards Cockmuir, taking a field track 150 metres past the farm, going SE towards Toxside. Just over 1km from Toxside take the left hand fork in the track and descend by the farm to a minor road. Continue on this road round the N side of Gladhouse Reservoir (formed in 1879) to Mauldslie. An old indistinct cart track goes off SE from between the cottages and the farm and follows a burn.

The track then becomes a sketchy path for 400 metres, but becomes distinct after it rounds a square wood and then ascends the face of Mauldslie Hill to the col between it and Torfichen Hill. In another 1½km the path, descending, joins a track and then the B7007 road. Cross this, go through a gate and continue directly over the moor (no path) to the Tathieknowe Burn. Follow this down on the right-hand bank, joining a track before Carcant, to reach the Heriot Water road 5km from Heriot.

This route is shown as a road on Armstrong's 1773 map of the Lothians, joining at Garvald the road from Edinburgh which came *via* Esperston and went S as the 'Traquair Road'.

From Heriot, the old Galashiels road goes NW over the hill to Middleton, 3km of it now being a grassy track.

41 Leadburn to Lyne
19¹/₂km/12mls   *Maps: OS 73/62; 2*

On the A703 road, 150 metres S of the crossroads at Leadburn, a path gives access to the dismantled railway. Follow the Peebles branch S to Waterhead. Bypass the gravel quarry by using the main road for some 800 metres, rejoin the old railway at the metal bridge and follow the line until it meets the road to Shiplaw. Go right along this road to the crossroads just W of Shiplaw. There turn left and continue S past Harehope and between Black Meldon and White Meldon to Lyne just N of the A72 road, 6¹/₂km from Peebles.

It is not necessary to use the public road at the Harehope Burn, as the track continues W and uphill from the public road and through a break in the forest to a picnic site.

It is possible to obtain access to this route at various points, including the convenient carpark about 1¹/₂km S of Leadburn on the A703 road and at Noblehouse on the A701, 8km SW of Leadburn. In the latter case (which has the advantage of joining the route S of the quarry section) follow the forest and farm road E to the crossroads W of Shiplaw and proceed to Lyne as above.

42 West Linton to Peebles
24km/15mls   *Maps: OS 72,73/62; 2*

Take the road SE by Broomlee to the Moffat road (A701) and go SW along this road for 800 metres. Then go uphill by Romanno House and SE over the hill to the Fingland Burn by a broad grassy track. On the S of Green Knowe at 186465 take the lower track and at 188461 (where a track leads round the hill to Fingland) take the footpath through a gate into the forest, across the stream and E through the forest to Greenside. From there go uphill, and in about 270 metres leave the main track and take the right-hand fork which goes up over the hill and descends to Upper Stewarton and Nether Stewarton. There go E to Mosshouse on the Lyne road, and S on this road for 530 metres; then turn left by the farm road to Upper Kidston. There go E up and around the N side of Hamilton Hill to a broad track leading SE to Peebles.

This route is the southward continuation of the drove road through the Cauldstane Slap (See routes 22 and 51). It is marked on Roy's map of 1755.

43 Peebles to Innerleithen

19½km/12mls   *Maps: OS 73/62; 2*

From the E side of Peebles Hydro a farm road goes N up the E side of the Soonhope Burn to Shieldgreen. The right of way passes in front of the house and immediately afterwards turns right and climbs steeply uphill past the ruin of Shieldgreen Tower, now a mound. The route is a broad, well-defined grassy track which crosses two forest roads and continues upwards, now on an easier gradient, to the col between Makeness Kipps and Dunslair Heights.

Continue in a northerly direction to a gap in the old stone dyke and then follow the break in the forest NE and then gently downhill for 150 metres to a forest road. There the original line of an old right of way down by the burn to Craighope has been obscured by forestry but, after a short section of rough steep ground, it is still possible to follow its general line by turning left along the forest road for 25 metres, then steeply down NE through a break in the forest to the upper end of the forest road which follows the burn down to Craighope. From there it is 9½km to Innerleithen.

An alternative route which avoids the steep section is to follow the track from the col to Dunslair Heights and from there take the forest road down to Williamslee.

44 Stow to Clovenfords

18km/11mls   *Maps: OS 73/62,69; 1*

From Stow cross the Gala Water to Stagehall and go S by road for 1½km, then go W by Lugate and Fowie to the col between Dunlee Hill and Scroof Hill. Descend to Scroof and go down the Caddon Water. Just after it turns E, go SE uphill over the NE shoulder of Black Law to Blackhaugh and down the Caddon Water by road to Clovenfords.

SECTION 4

The Pentland Hills

45 Colinton to Glencorse by Howden Glen
10km/6mls   *Maps: OS 66/62; 2*

Start from Dreghorn Loan by a new path which skirts the grounds of Laverockdale House and follows the Bonaly Burn under the city bypass road (A720). Thereafter bear left across a field to a gate and track which, after Green Craig Cistern, joins a distinct path up Howden Glen. This becomes a track as it crosses the pass between Allermuir Hill and Capelaw Hill, and continues S over Fala Knowe and downhill across the E side of Castlelaw Hill. The route continues past a prehistoric fort and souterrain and reaches Castlelaw Farm. Finally, go by Crosshouse and Glencorse Old Church to Milton Bridge on the A766 road.

Note: The Ministry of Defence own much of the land covered by this path and have a firing range S of Castlelaw Hill. When red flags are flying (red lights at night) walkers are not allowed into the area marked 'Danger Zone' on maps. The Pentland Hills walking map is advised.

46 Colinton to Glencorse by Bonaly
10km/6mls   *Maps: OS 66/62; 2*

From Colinton go up Bonaly Road, over the city bypass, and past Bonaly Tower to the entrance to Bonaly Park, where there is a carpark. Continue up the steep track past Bonaly Reservoir, over the col between Capelaw Hill and Harbour Hill and down to Glencorse Reservoir. Go left along the road to Flotterstone on the A702 road, and then by Glencorse Old Church to Milton Bridge.

47 Currie or Balerno to Glencorse
10km/6mls   *Maps: OS 66/62; 2*

From Currie go uphill on the Kirkgate road, passing the church, and continue straight on up to the moor. Then go SE through the Maiden's Cleuch, between Harbour Hill and Bell's Hill, and descend to Glencorse Reservoir where route 46 is joined. This route is shown on Roy's map of 1755.

Alternatively, starting from Balerno, go up Harlaw Road by Malleny Mills to the small track opposite Harlaw Farm (carpark). Bearing away from Harlaw Reservoir, continue almost due E across the moor to join the route from Currie before the climb to the Maiden's Cleuch pass.

By turning right at Glencorse Reservoir, routes 46 and 47 can be linked with route 48 by way of the road along Loganlee Reservoir.

48 Balerno to Penicuik by the Kirk Road

12km/7¹/₂mls   *Maps: OS 66/62; 2*

Take Mansfield Road from Balerno, passing Upper Dean Park Farm and Marchbank. Take the left fork at Red Moss Nature Reserve (carpark on left) and go straight on across Threipmuir Reservoir up the steep avenue past Bavelaw Castle, which is now a private residence. After a gate/stile, the route becomes a footpath going ESE and into Green Cleuch between Black Hill and Hare Hill to reach the Logan Burn. Follow the glen round to a cottage, The Howe, and just W of it a path goes steeply uphill over the high pass between Carnethy Hill and Scald Law (579m) – the highest of the Pentlands. This path is the Kirk Road to Penicuick. Continue downhill from the pass by the Grain Burn to the A702 road, turn left there and take the first road on the right which goes down by Coates Farm to Penicuick.

Note: Both Bavelaw and Loganlee are in Penicuick parish, and this was once the road to church for people living there.

By continuing E at The Howe, instead of climbing the Kirk Road, a narrow road leads by Loganlee and Glencorse reservoirs to join with routes 46 and 47.

49 Balerno to Nine Mile Burn by the Monks Road

10km/6mls   *Maps: OS 65 or 66/62; 2*

Follow route 48 to the top of the avenue at Bavelaw. Turn right then left to go S over the W shoulder of Hare Hill, then downhill slightly to cross the source of the Logan Burn in the Kitchen Moss.

From there climb E to the col on the SW side of West Kip. From that point there are three possible routes:

(a) by the Monks Road, uphill to the right over Cap Law and the Monks Rig and past the Font Stone to Nine Mile Burn.

(b) downhill to the right by a plantation and Braid Law to Nine Mile Burn.

(c) downhill to the left by Eastside Farm to Eight Mile Burn on the A702 road.

From the col on the SW side of West Kip a fourth route is often taken, a ridge walk going E along the spine of the Pentlands over West Kip, East Kip, Scald Law, Carnethy Hill and Turnhouse Hill to reach Flotterstone on the A702 road.

50 Balerno to Carlops by the Bore Stane
14km/9mls   *Maps: OS 65,66/62; 2*

Follow route 48 to Marchbank and then take the right fork at Red Moss Nature Reserve to follow the road by East Rigg which continues in a straight line as a path to Lintonshiels. This point can also be reached by road from the A70 4km W of Balerno. At Listonshiels turn S uphill to the Bore (Boar) Stone and then descend by the North Esk Reservoir to Carlops.

From Fairliehope, 1½km S of the reservoir, a short cut is provided by a path going down to the River North Esk (footbridge), and along its E bank to Carlops. From the S end of the reservoir another path goes E over the col between Spittal Hill and Patie's Hill to Spittal Farm and Nine Mile Burn.

51 Mid Calder to West Linton by the Cauldstane Slap
19km/12mls   *Maps: OS 65/62; 2*

From Mid Calder go SE through East Calder to the Lanark road (A70), and SW along this road for 1km to the path on the left beyond Little Vantage where a signpost indicates the route to West Linton. This path descends to cross the Water of Leith (footbridge) and then climbs very gradually to the pass known as the Cauldstane Slap. 1km S of the pass the path becomes a track which goes down to Baddinsgill Reservoir, from the S end of which a road continues down to West Linton.

At about 1km from the end of the reservoir a signpost beside the road indicates a path going off to the left to cross the Lyne Water (footbridge) to a track going by Stonypath to West Linton. Roy's map calls this route the 'Road to Queensferry'. It is an old drove road, and continues S to Peebles and St Mary's Loch by routes 42 and 22.

52 West Calder to Dolphinton
22km/14mls   *Maps: OS 65,72/62; 2*
From West Calder a road goes SE by Harburn and past the Roman camp at Castle Greg to the A70. Turn S there for ¹/₂km, taking the minor road on the left at a signpost. Leave this minor road, go S (keeping to the E of Mid Crosswood Farm) and then go SSE uphill to a signpost on the E shoulder of Henshaw Hill. Another right of way path joins the route at this point, coming from the A70 (Tarbrax road end) by the Dry Burn. Descend to cross the Garval Syke, then climb to the col between Darlees Hill and White Craig and cross the high bare moor to Black Law, where there is the grave of a Covenanter fatally wounded at Rullion Green in 1666.
From there continue SE and either:
(a) go left along a wide track at the foot of Black Law to West Linton, or
(b) continue S over the moor to the West Water and either follow its E bank to Garvald 3km from Dolphinton, or cross to Easton Farm and Dunsyre, or
(c) at a signpost ¹/₂km from the track go E to cross the Medwin Water to Medwynhead and follow the road by Ferniehaugh to Garvald, and go left along a wide track at the foot of Black Law to West Linton.

53 Auchengray to West Linton
20km/12¹/₂mls   *Maps: OS 65,72/61,62; 2*
From Auchengray go 2km S by road, then E by the farm road past East Yardhouses to the Old Lanark Road (A70). The route continues by a path going SE through a small plantation (take the left fork) and then by a clear track to Left Law. Then go E over the moor between Bleak Law and Mid Hill and NE across the West Water to a track which crosses the Medwin Water N of Medwynhead. Continue E

along this track to North Slipperfield and follow the road from there to West Linton.

From Left Law an alternative route goes S by Stonypath to the road 1½km W of Dunsyre. From there another road goes NE by Walton, Ferniehaugh and Cairn Muir to North Slipperfield and West Linton.

54 Carlops to Dolphinton
10km/6mls   *Maps: OS 65,72/62; 2*

This route follows a section of the Old Biggar Road. It starts on the W side of the A702 road just S of Carlops and goes SW by Linton Muir, West Linton Golf Course, Hardgatehead and Ingraston to Dolphinton. It goes partly along the line of a Roman road.

SECTION 5
Clydesdale and the Lowther Hills

PLACES OF INTEREST
Wanlockhead: Museum of Scottish lead mining
                 Lead mine visit
                 Beam engine, Merrockhan water tunnel (1763)
Leadhills: World's oldest lending library
                 Grave of Scotland's oldest man
Between Leadhills and Wanlockhead there is a narrow gauge railway (usually working at weekends).

55 Lamington to Broughton
19km/12mls   *Maps: OS 72/68;* **2**
Take the road which starts just S of Lamington church and leads SE to Baitlaws. Just before reaching there, branch off left by a farm road which descends to cross the Lamington Burn and then goes uphill to Cowgill Loch. Continue to Cowgill from where a road goes to Birthwood and down the Culter Water. At Snaip turn off this road, go past Nisbet Farm and when the track forks take the right-hand one to Cow Castle. From there go E through the gap between March Brae and White Hill, past a derelict cottage on the right-hand side, to reach Kilbucho old church, Mitchell Hill and the road to Broughton.

56 Coulter to Crawford
20km/12½mls   *Maps: OS 72/68;* **2**
From Coulter take the road S up Culter Water, and when it forks in 3km take the right fork which goes past Birthwood. In about 1km, and shortly after two bridges are crossed, (at 019304 where there is car parking) follow the path which climbs SSW over Cowgill Rig and leads down towards the ruin of Windgate House near the SE corner of Cowgill Upper Reservoir. From the ruin go SE up the steep

slope to the col between Windgate Bank and Hudderstone. From there descend SSE by the Linn Burn to the road down Grains Burn, and continue along it on the W side of Camps Reservoir, and finally down the Camps Water to Crawford.

From the road junction at 019304 to Windgate House an alternative route goes up the road past Cowgill Lower Reservoir to the dam on Cowgill Upper Reservoir. Continue along the E side of this reservoir, difficult going with no visible path, to the ruin of Windgate House and continue as above.

57 Beattock Summit to Moffat
18km/11mls   *Maps: OS 78/68; 2*

From a point 1½km NW of Beattock Summit and just off the M74 motorway at 983160, where a sign points to 'Bodsberry Cottage and Little Clyde', take the metalled road E for 1½km past a cottage and then follow an old track SE through the forest for another 1½km. Just before reaching Upper Howecleugh fork left round the foot of Nap Hill, then drop down to the Fopperbeck Burn at a ford and ascend SE through the forest on the course of a Roman road to skirt Erickstane Hill in an easterly direction to a fork in the track. At a small upright wooden construction (039139) turn SE along a cleared strip (buried gas pipelines) for 1½km to a stream at a dip in the track. At this point the old right of way (Roman road) also crosses the track at 047127. Turn left (SE) and follow the right of way (and stream) over rough ground for 200 metres. The way ahead then crosses another forestry track at a small pond.

Continue SE on the right of way up a clearing in the forest and through a low col to descend steeply to the A701 road. Crossing this (1½km S of the Devil's Beef Tub) continue the descent by the old road to join the valley road at Ericstane 6km N of Moffat. (From the point where the A701 is crossed, the line of the Roman road is due S on the high ground – see OS map).

58 Roberton to Douglas
14km/9mls   *Maps: OS 72/68; 2*

Go up the Roberton Burn to Nap Bridge and in another 160 metres look on the left for the old drove road going NW across the moor on the N side of the Roberton Burn to Fallside. From there continue W by road for 1km to Bodinglee, and then by a path (only visible in places) SW then W across the slopes of Bodinglee Law to Maidengill. From there go down to the M74 motorway by a track which goes under the motorway to reach the B7078 road (formerly the A74). Go N up this road for 1km to Parkhead Cottage and from there go W past the S end of a wood (path just discernible) to the A70 road 800 metres NE of Douglas.

59 Douglas to Wanlockhead
23km/14½mls   *Maps: OS 71/68; 2*
   Go up Springhill Road, passing on the E of Springhill Farm, to Pagie Hill and SE across pathless moorland between Auchensaugh Hill and Mid Rig to Crawfordjohn. There cross the Duneaton Water and go S by road to Glentewing and then by path to Holmhead. Continue up the Snar Water to Snarhead, where it is preferable to take the track which goes SE over Hunt Law before dropping down to Leadhills, 1½km by road from Wanlockhead.
   Note: On Roy's map of 1755 the first part of this route to Crawfordjohn is shown as a road.

60 Muirkirk to Wanlockhead
32km/20mls   *Maps: OS 71/67,68; 1,2*
   This old drove road goes S from Muirkirk past Kames and up the Garpel Water to the col (410m) between Wardlaw Hill and Stony Hill. Continuing SE then E, the path, boggy in places, enters the forest on the SE slope of Drummond's Knowe. A forest road leads on to Fingland, and from there the line of the old drove road goes E up the slopes on the S side of Spango Water. 1½km E of Fingland the track peters out and is picked up again on the N side of Shiel Hill at a height of almost 430m.
   Continue over Peat Rig and descend to Spango Bridge on the B740 road between Sanquhar and Crawfordjohn. From a point 400 metres NE of Spango Bridge go SE by Clackleith and follow a track through the forest round the S side of Duntercleugh Rig (where the Southern Upland Way is joined) to descend to Duntercleugh and continue up the Wanlock Water to Wanlockhead.

61 Muirkirk to Kirkconnel
21km/13mls   *Maps: OS 71/67,68;* **1,2**

Follow route 60 as far as Fingland, then go SW by road up the Glengap Burn for 1½km. Leave the road just before it turns E and continue SW over the col and down the slopes of Kirkland Hill above Glenaylmer Burn to Kirkland and Kirkconnel.

62 Wanlockhead to Sanquhar
13km/8mls   *Maps: OS 71/68;* **2**

(a) From W of Wanlockhead the track up Black Hill can only be seen for a short distance. Keep uphill, over the ridge on the right and round the head of a rocky valley where a track across the grass marks the route to Stood Hill. From Stood Hill a new fence can be followed above the valley W to Willowgrain Hill and from there continue W along the crest of the hill and downwards to the N end of a wood to join the Southern Upland Way near Bogg, 2½km by road from Sanquhar.

(b) Alternative: Take the road going NW down Wanlock Water past Wanlockhead cemetery for 2½km. Cross the Wanlock Water and go up Glengaber Hill by a track which crosses the ridge NW of the summit and goes SW down to Cogshead. From there climb SW over the col to the SE of Conrig Hill and continue in the same direction downhill towards the N end of the wood near Bogg as in (a). This route follows part of the Southern Upland Way.

Note: Route (b) is recommended in the lambing and grouse shooting seasons.

63 Wanlockhead to Enterkinfoot by the Enterkin Pass
11km/7mls   *Maps: OS 78/68;* **2**

On the E side of Wanlockhead a signpost at 876129 marks the right of way leading SE up the W side of Stake Hill. In 1km it joins the road to the radar station, and leaves it again after 500 metres to continue due S to the Enterkin Pass (882106) between Lowther Hill and Fast Mount Lowther. From the pass there is a choice of two routes to Enterkinfoot:

(a) Descend by the W bank of the Enterkin Burn for 3km until it turns W at Glenvalentine. From there climb S up the track from the burn to the ridge ahead. Keep going S down this ridge (with spectacular views of Enterkin Glen) to join the metalled road near Inglestone. Continue by the public road *via* Muiryhill, turning W to the A76 Nithsdale road and Enterkinfoot. (To reach Durisdeermill, turn E immediately on reaching the road near Inglestone and take the track to Eastside to join the A702 Dalveen Pass road).

(b) From the Enterkin Pass another path goes SW, traversing along the W side of East Mount Lowther for 1½km, then dropping to the col (525m) between it and Threehope Height. Descend S by a spur to cross the Auchenlone Burn and continue S over the col between Cairn Hill and Coshogle Rig and then down by Kirkbride to Enterkinfoot.

Note: The two routes (a) and (b) can be combined as a circuit (22km/14mls).

64 Daer Reservoir to Durisdeer

14km/8½mls   Maps: OS 78/68; **2**

From the A702 take the road to the Daer Reservoir for 5km to Kirkhope Cleuch (967073), where there is good parking. From there two routes are possible:

(a) Proceed S for 5km past Kirkhope and SW up Thick Cleuch, over the col and down Tansley Burn. At 924008 (where the Tansley Burn joins Berry Grain) turn NW through a pass to the Glenleith Burn and continue NW by a track down Glenaggart to Durisdeer.

(b) A much shorter and more direct route goes up Kirkhope Cleuch for 3km to the col between Comb Law and Hirstane Rig, then SW by the Well Path between Well Hill and Durisdeer Hill and down the Kirk Burn to Durisdeer.

Part of this route was originally a Roman road, and in the Middle Ages was the road between Clydesdale and Nithsdale and the route to Galloway used by James IV on his pilgrimages to the shrine of St Ninian at Whithorn. The Lord High Treasurer's Accounts for 1497 contain an item "to the wife of Durisdeer, where the King lodged, 14s". The King's route was by Biggar, Cold Chapel (near Abington), Crawford Muir, Durisdeer, Penpont and Dalry.

Note: In a building behind Durisdeer Church (open all year) are the Queensberry Marbles.

65 Daer Reservoir to Thornhill

22km/13¹/₂mls   *Maps: OS 78/68; 2*

(a) From the Daer Reservoir proceed as in route 64(a) to the junction of the Tansley Burn and Berry Grain at 924008 where there is a choice of (i) continuing SW by Cample Cleuch to Burn Farm; or (ii) going W round Par Hill by a track high above Kettleton Reservoir to Burn Farm and thence by road to Thornhill.

(b) From the Daer Reservoir go S to Kirkhope and continue by a track up the valley to Daerhead. Continue almost due S to the col on W side of Earncraig Hill and descend on the S side to Burleywhag. At that point there is a choice of two routes: (i) Go down the W side of the Capel Burn to Locherben, then go W by road to Thornhill; or (ii) take the track past a bothy and down the E side of the Capel Burn to Mitchellslacks and from there go by road to Thornhill. There is no clear track from Mitchellslacks W over Threip Moor to Dollard. The road by Loch Ettrick and Closeburn is a picturesque, though rather long, route to Thornhill.

A circular route is possible using route (i) above as far as Locherben, then going NW by track and path up the Garroch Water and over the col at its head to reach the Tansley Burn and return from there to Daer Reservoir by Thick Cleuch (route 64a in reverse).

66 Ae Village to Beattock by the Forest of Ae

21km/13mls   *Maps: OS 78/68,74; 2*

From Ae Bridgend on the A701 Beattock to Dumfries road (bus route) a public road goes NW to Ae Village. 1¹/₂km beyond the village a forest road strikes off to the right and goes up the W bank of the Water of Ae for 3km to cross a bridge and continue up the E bank, still rising steadily along a forest track for 5km in a N direction to the forest boundary (and gate) at 017974. Head NW for 1km following the ditch in a narrow forest ride to 012981. Then resume NE along a contouring track for about 2km to cross the ridge to Lochanhead, from where a road runs NE by Kinnelhead and Earshaig to Beattock.

Note: Forestry developments may take place between the Forest of Ae and Lochanhead. If this happens, it is hoped that any new routes will be signposted.

SECTION 6
Galloway and Ayrshire

67 Ballantrae to New Luce or Stranraer
27km/17mls   *Maps: OS 76,82/72,79; 3*

Cross the River Stinchar and after 1km go E uphill past Kilwhannel, over the NE shoulder of Smirton Hill, then over Beneraird at a height of 424m. Continue to Lagafater Lodge and down the Water of Luce by Barnvannoch and High Mark to New Luce. (1km N of Barnvannoch another track goes S over the Water of Luce to Glenwhilly).

Alternative: To reach Stranraer take the road about 1km south of High Mark to Penwhirn Reservoir, and then SW over Braid Fell to Innermessan, 4km by road from Stranraer.

68 Girvan to Barr
11km/8mls   *Maps: OS 76/72; 3*

At the roundabout on the main road on the S of Girvan go due E uphill over the railway and continue along a track, then a path by Laggan Loch over to Barbae and Tormitchell. From there go to Dupin, and E over Auchensoul Hill to Barr.

69 Barr to Barrhill
18km/11mls   *Maps: OS 76/72; 3*

From Barr go by road to Alton Albany Farm, then strike uphill to White Knowes. Continue S for 1km uphill and change direction SSE (at 273911) to ascend to the col between West Hill and Mid Scalloch. Enter the forest at the NE corner of the loch (at 285891) and go along a track in the same direction through the forest for 4km to reach White Clauchrie. Proceed S by a forest ride for a clear route to Black Clauchrie. From there a farm road goes WSW to Darnaconnar and Laggan to reach the A714 road at Blair Farm, 1km SE of Barrhill.

70 Barr to Kirriereoch and Bargrennan
16km/10mls and 25km/16mls　　　　*Maps: OS 76,77/72,73; 3*

(a) From Barr go SE to the E side of Dinmurchie Loch, then keep round the forest fence until 160m E of the corner where the line of the track is picked up again. After crossing the Water of Gregg the track is clear to the ruins of Darley; the next stage, with little or no track, is to ascend to the NE shoulder of Cairn Hill, high above the Lead Mine Burn, and go SE through the Nick of Darley. On the far side descend by the Fardin Burn (with the forest on your left) to the second ride. There turn E along it until in about 400 metres a forest road is joined. In about 1km, when the road forks at 326896, keep left (E) to the Bargrennan road which is reached about 800m S of Rowantree fork and 2½km N of Kirriereoch.

The first part of this route is shown as a road on Armstrong's 1773 map of Ayrshire. A note on the map reads "At the Nick of Darlae and half a mile west the Road leads on the side of a very steep Hill, it's not above two feet broad and if you stumble you must fall almost Perpendicular six or seven hundred Feet".

(b) An alternative route to Bargrennan from the fork in (a) at 326896 is to take the right-hand forest road and follow it S for about 3km to Fardin (ruin). There go left (E) for about 460 metres; then take another forest road which branches right (S) across the River Cree and in 7km reaches the A714 about 5km NW of Bargrennan.

71 Pinwherry to Kirriereoch
22½km/14mls　　　　*Maps: OS 76,77/72,73; 3*

Take the road SE to Liglartrie, then go NE by the minor road *via* Docherniel and Mark to the Muck Water, where it ends. (Mark can also be reached by a road from Pinmore Mains, 5km N of Pinwherry). From Muck Water a forest road leads SE through the forest to Shalloch Well, and then E to White Clauchrie, Ferter, Fardin and Kirriereoch.

72 Barrhill to Kirriereoch
16km/10mls　　　　*Maps: OS 76,77/72,73; 3*

From Barrhill take the A714 road towards Newton Stewart for 1km to Blair Farm. Turn left onto the road signposted 'Footpath by

Black Clauchrie' and follow this road NE by Laggan and
Darnaconnar. At Black Clauchrie the road ends and a track
continues NE for 2km further. The track enters a forest ride which is
followed for about 1km until the end of a forest road appears on the
left. Some 40 metres beyond there the track becomes indistinct; veer
to the right, cross a small bridge towards the Fardin Burn, ford it at
the remains of a bridge and continue directly ahead down a forest
ride to join the forest road. Turn right past Fardin to Kirriereoch.

73 Newton Stewart to Bargrennan via Loch Dee
29km/18mls   *Maps: OS 77,83/73; 3*
    Go through Minigaff and NE to Kirkland and Glenhoise by road,
then left by the road over the Penkiln Burn and up the burn to
Auchinleck. Continue by forest road to Drigmorn, and then go up
the E side of the Pulnee Burn to a rough but well-defined path
leading through the gap between Curlywee and Millfore to White
Laggan Bothy. 400 metres beyond the bothy is the Southern Upland
Way, running W to E. The way E is described in route 78. Turning
W towards Glentrool, follow the waymarkers, until 5km beyond
White Laggan Bothy there is a choice of either:
    (a) following the Southern Upland Way on the S side of Loch
Trool to Bargrennan, or
    (b) crossing Glenhead Burn to the road and going along the N
side of Loch Trool to Glentrool Village and on to Bargrennan.

74 Newton Stewart to New Galloway (by the Old Edinburgh
Road) or Dalry
29km/18mls   *Maps: OS 77,83/73; 3*
    The line of this old road, long since unused, is marked on the OS
map. It goes N from Minigaff to Kirkland; then in another 1km the
modern road goes left whilst a section of the old road runs from
424674 for 3km to meet a forestry road, which is best joined at
463690, and continues by Loch of the Lowes to Black Loch. Next
comes an open section, and then a forest road not quite on the line
of the old road to Clatteringshaws. Beyond this, the Old Edinburgh
Road can be picked up again at 570772. There go E, at first through
forest, to New Galloway. Alternatively, go NE by a forest road and
then between Glenlee Hill and Maggot Hill to Dalry.

White Laggan bothy near Loch Dee (routes 73 and 78)

The Girvan Valley at Straiton from Sclenteuch Moor (route 85)

Looking east from the Bealach nan Corp towards Balquhidder (route 116)

The right of way between Tyndrum and Glen Lyon (route 140)

75 Polmaddie to Carsphairn (The Polmaddie Trail)

7km/4¹/₂mls   *Maps: OS 77/73; 3*

From the A713 road 2km N of Carsfad Loch locate the track going WSW between the footbridge over the Polmaddy Burn and the first building in the ruined village of Polmaddie. Go past a carpark and then head NW on an old pack road through young forest on the W side of the Polmaddy Burn for about 4km. After crossing the burn turn right along the track on the E side of Gairy Craig. Leave the forest at Braidenoch and go N across the slopes of Bardennoch Hill to reach Carnavel and the A713 road at the bridge over the Water of Deugh 1km SE of Carsphairn.

76 Clatteringshaws to Mossdale (The Raiders Road)

14¹/₂km/9mls   *Maps: OS 77/73; 3*

Start from the N side of the bridge which carries the A712 road over the River Dee where it flows out of Clatteringshaws Loch, and follow a forest road on the N bank of the Dee SE for 13km to Stroan Loch. At the old railway viaduct a forest road turns N and in 400 metres a gate on the right leads to a path to Mossdale.

77 Glentrool Village to Merrick

13km/8mls   *Maps: OS 77/73; 3*

Go by the minor road up Glen Trool to the Bruce Stone, then N up the Buchan Burn to Culsharg bothy. From there the route goes NW uphill just on the N side of the Forestry Commission bridge and leads to the dyke which passes right over Benyellary to the W shoulder of Merrick (843m). The return from Culsharg can be made through the forest by a road which leads to Stroan Bridge, 1km from Glentrool Village.

78 Bargrennan to Dalry by Clatteringshaws

42km/26mls   *Maps: OS 77/73; 3*

This is the fourth section of the Southern Upland Way which leaves the A714 road at Bargrennan opposite the village hall and strikes E over the hill to a bridge over the Water of Minnoch. It then goes up Glen Trool by the S side of Loch Trool, past Caldons caravan site (shop) and at Glenhead it is joined by an alternative route on the N side of Loch Trool. 4km beyond Glenhead is Loch

Dee and White Laggan Bothy. Continuing E, the Southern Upland Way crosses the Black Water of Dee, goes downstream to Clatteringshaws Loch and then crosses the hills NNE at first to Clenrie, then E to Dalry. The official Southern Upland Way map is particularly useful for this route.

79 Bargrennan to Dalry by Backhill of Bush
39km/24mls   *Maps: OS 77/73; 3*
   Go up Glen Trool on the N side of Loch Trool past the Bruce Stone to Buchan. From there take the path ENE up the hillside to the Gairland Burn and ascend beside this to Loch Valley. Beyond this loch go NE around the E side of Loch Neldricken, then N for 1km and turn E over the ridge (494m) between Craignaw and Dungeon Hill to the Round Loch of the Dungeon.
   In order to avoid the dangerous Silver Flowe bog on the S side of this loch, go round its N side. Watch carefully for sound footing across the very boggy ground. Follow the forest boundary SE to 474843 where the route meets the ride at the edge of the forest leading to Backhill of Bush (bothy).
   From the bothy follow a track NNE for 800 metres to 483851 and turn right by the uphill track for another 800 metres to 496850. Then go NE directly up a steep slope to cross a col (628m) on the Rhinns of Kells, and descend steeply ESE across Hawse Burn (above the waterfall) into the forest and past a shepherd's memorial. Then go due E by a forest ride and tracks midway between Loch Minnoch and Loch Dungeon to join (at 543846) a track turning NE *via* Burnhead to the end of a minor public road. Go down it for 6½km to Polharrow Bridge, and a further 3½km to Dalry.

80 Bargrennan to Carsphairn or Dalmellington
39km/24mls   *Maps: OS 77/73; 3*
   Follow route 79 to Backhill of Bush. Go N along a forest road for 2km and contour round Little Craigtarson to reach Riders Rig in 3km at 480883. From there strike NW along a forest ride, taking the fourth ride on the right going NE to meet another forest road on the E side of Gala Lane leading to Loch Head. From there strike uphill by the E bank of the Loch Head Burn for about 1km, swinging ENE and heading for the pass out of the forest to 503922. Turn N over

the top of Bow (612m) to the next col S of Coran of Portmark (662m), then head ENE down a steep slope to reach the disused mines beside the Garryhorn Burn. From there go E along the track past Garryhorn to reach the A731 road 1½ km N of Carsphairn.

(b) Alternative from Backhill of Bush. Follow route 79 to the col (628m) on the Rhinns of Kells. Then go N over Corserine (814m), Carlin's Cairn, and Meaul (695m) to Bow and the col S of Coran of Portmark, and from there descend as in route 80(a) to Carsphairn.

(c) Alternative from the head of Loch Doon to Dalmellington. Cross the Gala Lane, take the road by Starr and turn N along the W bank of Loch Doon. 800 metres beyond the end of the loch go left at Caw Glen Burn to Bellsbank and Dalmellington.

81 Bargrennan to Dalmellington by Tunskeen
43km/27mls   *Maps: OS 77/67,73; 3*

Go by road up Glen Trool to the Buchan Burn, and up this burn to Culsharg bothy. 200 metres beyond it turn right onto a forest track and go up by the NW bank of the Buchan Burn for 2km to leave the forest at 430836. Continue NE to the SW corner of Loch Enoch, go along its W side and then head NNW on the lower slopes of Kirriereoch Hill (no path, rough and boggy) and cross Castle on Oyne to Tunskeen bothy. Continue N, keeping W of the forest fence until a track is reached at 424916 below the ruins of Slaethornrig. Follow this track above the W side of Loch Riecawr, and just beyond this loch join a forest road where two alternatives are:

(a) go E to Loch Doon and along its W side to Dalmellington,

(b) go NW to the S end of Loch Bradan and then W to Stinchar Bridge, and 2km N of there join route 84 to Dalmellington.

82 Clatteringshaws Loch to Dalmellington
38½km/24mls   *Maps: OS 77/73; 3*

From the A712 Newton Stewart road, 8km W of New Galloway, a forest road strikes NW to Upper Craigenbay. In 1km further the Southern Upland Way is joined and followed S for 1km to the edge of Clatteringshaws Loch, then 4km W to the point where the Way crosses the Black Water of Dee at 495794. At that point do not cross the river, but go NW then N along a forest track to reach Backhill of Bush in 6km and join route 80 to Dalmellington.

83 Barr to Carsphairn
39km/24mls   *Maps: OS 76,77/67,73;* **3**

From Barr take the road up the Water of Gregg for about 1½km, and fork left at the forestry offices up the side of a wood to High Changue, and thence E through the forest to Balloch Hill. There the forest road turns N downhill and then NW to join the public road near Clashgulloch Farm. (If time is short, this point can be reached by the public road from Barr).

Now go E to North Balloch, and E from there by a forest road which after about 1½km goes up by the Whiterow Burn to the N side of Dunamoddie and over Eldrick Hill before turning SE to the River Stinchar. Where the river bends SE, strike E for 1km to the Straiton road, 1½km N of Stinchar Bridge, then S along this road to the bridge. From it a metalled road goes E to 417960, then a forest road leads by Ballochbeatties and the N side of Loch Riecawr to Loch Doon. Finally, go from Loch Head at the head of the loch to Carsphairn as in the last part of route 80a.

84 Barr to Dalmellington
31km/19mls   *Maps: OS 76,77/72,67;* **3**

Follow route 83 until the Straiton road is reached. Then go N for 1½km (400 metres past Talaminnoch), and turn off E by a forest road (gate 202) through Tairlaw Plantation to Knockdon on the Water of Girvan. From Knockdon Farm go uphill by the E side of the burn. Cross the moor to the S and E of Widow's Loch and Black Loch to Little Shalloch. A tractor track is followed to Nether Berbeth (ruin), from where a road joins the B741 at the bridge over the River Doon 2km from Dalmellington.

85 Barr to Straiton and Patna
21km/13mls   *Maps: OS 76,77/67,73;* **3**

Follow route 83 as far as North Balloch, then go N for 1km to the Dalquhairn Burn and head NE up its N side for 1½km to enter a young forest. 500 metres further upstream at 347978 make a diversion (450 metres E then 400 metres N) to continue NE by a track crossing the shoulder of Garleffin Fell. Leave the forest at 362992 and continue *via* Palmullan Burn and down the W side of the Water of Girvan to Straiton.

Continue from a point ½km up the B741 road to Dalmellington, where a minor road leads NE uphill to a track through young trees and over Sclenteuch Moor to Dhu Loch Cottage (ruin).

The last 4km to Patna through forest needs two diversions to avoid encroaching trees. Enter the plantation by the left-hand ride, heading N and NNE to the E end of Loch Spallander, where it crosses an E to W ride. Then, at 399082, bear NW to reach a path and dry-stane dyke leading NE up Glenside Hill to another dyke. Follow this one NNW down to the Backglen Burn at 398091, then go NE to rejoin the track over the ridge to Patna.

86 Dalry to Sanquhar
43km/27mls   *Maps: OS 77,78/67,68;* **2,3**
In Dalry go up the main street to the left fork beyond the B7000 road, then go NE by Ardoch Hill to Butterhole Bridge, and over Culmark Hill to the B729 road at Stroanfreggan. Go E there for 250 metres, then turn left NE up Manquhill Hill to Benbrack (580m) on the watershed. On the E slope the Southern Upland Way is at first partly through forests (where the official map is essential for route-finding) until a tarred road is joined at Polskeoch. This road is followed for 3½km and is left at Polgown where the Southern Upland Way strikes left to the NE and leads over Cloud Hill and down into the Nith Valley at Sanquhar.

87 New Cumnock to Dalry by Glen Afton
42km/26mls   *Maps: OS 71,77/67,73;* **3**
Follow the road S up Glen Afton to Afton Reservoir, and then continue above the plantation on its W bank to the S end. There keep S up the Afton Water and over the col on the W of Alhang, then down the Holm Burn, across it to the path on the slope of Mid Hill of Glenhead, and down the glen to Dalquhairn.

From there go SW down the Water of Ken by the road to Strahanna, and then strike due S up the hillside by a forest track to Meikle Auchrae and S to join the Southern Upland Way 1km before reaching Stroanpatrick. Continue S by Culmark Hill, Butterhole Bridge and Ardoch to Dalry. (This route is shown as a road in 1773 on Armstrong's map of Ayrshire).

SECTION 7
Arran

88 Brodick to Sannox (and Corrie) via Glen Rosa
14½km/9mls   *Maps: OS 69/66; 3*

This route goes through some of the grandest mountain scenery in Arran. The first 2km from Brodick are by road to Glenrosa Farm. From there the path is on the W side of the Glenrosa Water, heading due N up Glen Rosa to the obvious pass of The Saddle between Cir Mhor and North Goatfell. The path is very clear, but at the point where it branches do not diverge NW into Fionn Choire. The final ascent to The Saddle is easy, but the descent on the N side of the pass is much steeper. A cairn about 100 metres NW of the lowest point of the pass indicates the start of the descent to an eroded dyke where care should be taken not to dislodge loose rock and rubble. Below this the way improves and there is the option of paths on both sides of the burn. The one on the right bank leads to an old barytes mine from where a track goes down to the road at Sannox. Corrie is a further 2½km S and there is an infrequent bus service back to Brodick.

89 Brodick to Lochranza via Glen Rosa
18km/11mls   *Maps: OS 69/66; 3*

From Brodick follow route 88 up Glen Rosa to the branching of paths at the foot of Fionn Choire. At that point take the left-hand path up this corrie, heading NNW then NW below the great granite spire of the Rosa Pinnacle to reach the col (560m) between Cir Mhor and A'Chir. On the NW side of this col descend quite steeply at first for a short distance, then make a long gradually descending traverse across the W side of Caisteal Abhail to reach the col at Loch na Davie. From there descend the path down Gleann Easan Biorach to Lochranza.

90 Lochranza to Machrie
20km/12½mls   *Maps: OS 69/66; 3*

The first part of this route goes up Gleann Easan Biorach, which starts at the SE end of Lochranza village. There is a path as far Loch na Davie at the pass leading to Glen Iorsa, but the descent of this glen is long and very hard going over wet and hummocky ground beside the Iorsa Water. Eventually a path is reached on the N side of Loch Iorsa, and it makes the last 3km to Dougrie easier. Machrie is 2km further S by road.

Alternative: Follow the coast road W from Lochranza for 4km through Catacol to the bridge at the foot of Glen Catacol. Go up this delightful glen by a path which fades out in boggy ground near the col at its head. Continue S past Loch Tanna and descend to Glen Iorsa where the preceding route is joined. This is 3km longer than the preceding route.

Another walk in the N of the island goes from Lochranza to the foot of Glen Catacol, then up this glen for 2km. Instead of going S to its head as described above, go SE up Gleann Diomhan and round the S of Beinn Bhreac, then N to Loch na Davie and down Gleann Easan Biorach to return to Lochranza (16km).

91 Lamlash to Lagg
15km/9½mls   *Maps: OS 69/66; 3*

A right of way goes from the Monamore Glen (2km SW of Lamlash) to Kilmory near Lagg at the SW corner of the island. It takes a fairly direct line, passing to the E of Urie Loch and crossing the moor E of Glas Choirein. Afforestation of much of the moorland in the SE corner of Arran has blocked this way and made it impracticable.

An alternative route by a forest road goes from the Monamore Glen at 015297, first SE then S to the Glenashdale Falls. This point can also be reached by a short walk from Whiting Bay. The road continues W then SW past Auchareoch and reaches the A841 1½km E of Lagg.

SECTION 8
Argyll

92 Dunoon (Glen Lean) to Loch Striven and Ardtaraig
17km/10^1/$_2$mls   *Maps: OS 63/59; 4*

Start from the A836 road through Glen Lean (6km NW of Dunoon) at the foot of Glen Kin. Follow the private road up the E side of Glen Kin past the cottages at Stronsaul. Continue a short distance towards Glenkin and after crossing the Glenkin Burn turn left along an old track through the forest which goes up the glen to join a newer road. Follow this road for 200 metres until it swings round NW crossing two streams. (This point can equally well be reached by walking up the forest road on the W side of Glen Kin). At the second stream take an indistinct path up the narrow clearing between stream and forest to a stile over an upper forest fence. There is no path up the grassy hillside beyond, but the going is easy to the flat Bealach na Sreine, where three fences meet. Descend W down grassy slopes to cross the stream in the Inverchaolain Glen, and go down the path on its W side to Loch Striven. Finally go N to the end of the road at Invergain and continue beyond there by the right of way to the A836 road at Ardtaraig.

Note: A convenient post bus from Dunoon goes past the start of this walk and via Ardtaraig on weekdays.

The next five routes are in the Argyll Forest Park.

93 Hunter's Quay (or the Younger Botanic Garden) to Strachur
27km/17mls   *Maps: OS 56,63/53,59; 4*

Go by the A815 road to the main entrance of the Younger Botanic Garden (carpark). If walking, there is an alternative road on the W side of the River Eachaig. Inside the garden go to Benmore Home Farm and continue N along a private road on the W side of Loch Eck. This road leads to Glenbranter, and beyond there another minor road continues to Strachur.

94 Ardentinny to Lochgoilhead
18km/11mls   *Maps: OS 56/53;* **4**

From Ardentinny go along the edge of Finart Bay by a private road and path to Stronvochlan. The walk may be started from this point where there is a carpark. At first go NW up a forest road behind Stronvochlan, and follow the road E, gradually descending to the shore of Loch Long. Continue along the lochside by a road which eventually climbs uphill to the prominent electricity transmission pylon. Continue uphill from it on a grassy track for a short distance, then turn N along a clearing through the forest by a waymarked path. After about ½km the path descends through natural oakwoods to the lochside. Go along the grassy fringe below the woods past Ardnahein to reach the road end 1km from Carrick Castle and 9km from Lochgoilhead.

95 Lochgoilhead to Invernoaden or Strachur by the Curra Lochain
10km/6½mls   *Maps: OS 56/53;* **4**

Start at Lettermay by the road entering the forest at 188999. Follow this road for just over 1km and then take the right fork descending slightly to cross the Lettermay Burn. Then go NNE for 200 metres on the E edge of the forest and enter it at a mound of rocks to reach a firebreak. Follow the upper right-hand firebreak SW along a path with marker posts past several obstacles formed by fallen trees and wet bog. Reach the E end of the Curra Lochain and continue more easily along its N side and over the grassy Bealach an Lochain. A few hundred metres beyond a small fank, go left through a clearing in the forest towards the Leavanin Burn and follow a faint path high on its N side. Cross the burn in a further 2km and reach the forest road on the NE side of Beinn Lagan. From there go S to Invernoaden or, alternatively, go NW round the N side of the hill to Strachur.

96 Lochgoilhead to Invernoaden by Lochain nan Cnaimh
11km/7mls   *Maps: OS 56/53;* **4**

Start at the same point as for route 95, but keep left after 1km and continue SW along the road and its continuation up a gradually rising path along a fire-break. Then climb steeply SE towards the outflow of Lochain nan Cnaimh. Go along the W shore of the lochan and follow a path which climbs steeply towards the col between Beinn Bheula and Croc na Tricriche. This part of the route is marked by posts across the col and down the grassy slopes of Coire Ealt to the upper edge of the Loch Eck Forest (much of it now felled). Turn right along the forest road to cross the Coire Ealt Burn and continue NW gradually downhill to the A815 road a short distance from Invernoaden.

Note: It is possible to combine routes 95 and 96 into a circular walk.

97 Arrochar to Lochgoilhead
10 – 19km/6 – 12mls   *Maps: OS 56/53; 4*
   (a) From Ardgartan camp site, 3km from Arrochar (bus), or from Ardgartan youth hostel, take the road S along the shore of Loch Long and continue by the forest road along the shore, above Coilessan and rising to the Corran Lochan above Mark. Then go N from this lochan for 2½km over the Ardgoil peninsula and descend towards Stuckbeg on Loch Goil. Reach Lochgoilhead by either the high forest road about 100m above the loch, or a lower track in bad condition which leads to a road along the shore of loch.
   (b) As (a) until just beyond Coilessan, then go up the Coilessan Glen and continue due W over the pass at 500m and descend to the Donich Water to join (c) to Lochgoilhead.
   (c) From Ardgartan, follow the forest track that goes W then NW beyond Creagdhu in Glen Croe, gradually climbing to about 230m. When close below the saddle between The Brack and Ben Donich, strike uphill and over the saddle (381m) and descend by a broad lane through the forest to the track on the SE side of the Donich Water. This leads down to Lochgoilhead.

98 Arrochar (Ardgartan) to Loch Sloy and Butterbridge
16km/10mls   *Maps: OS 56/53; 4*
   From Arrochar go up the E side of Glen Loin, by road at first, then due N under the transmission lines to Inveruglas Water and the Hydro Electric road to the Loch Sloy dam. From the dam follow a path along the difficult W side of the loch almost to its head, then

go W to a private road which leads SW down Glen Kinglas to Butterbridge on the A83 road. The return to Arrochar may be made by bus, or by walking up to the Rest and be Thankful and down the old road in Glen Croe.

99 Loch Fyne to Glen Falloch
17km/11mls   *Maps: OS 56/53;* **4**
   (a) From the head of Loch Fyne at 194125 walk along the private road up Glen Fyne to the bridge just beyond Glenfyne Lodge. Cross to the E side of the river and continue up the road to the reservoir on the Allt na Lairige. Go along the S side of the reservoir and continue by pathless and boggy ground over the Lairig Arnan, and down the N side of the Allt Arnan to the end of another road, which leads down to Glenfalloch Farm 1½km N of Inverarnan. It is possible to make a shorter descent from this road by descending along the N side of the Allt Arnan direct to Inverarnan.
   (b) An alternative and slightly longer route (20km/13mls) goes right up Glen Fyne to the end of the path 3km/2mls beyond Inverchorachan. Leave the glen just beyond this point and go E along the Allt Coir'an Longairt for 3km to reach the Hydro Electric road in Gleann nan Caorann, and walk down this to Glenfalloch Farm.
   (c) Another much longer route is from Inveraray (34km/22mls). Go 2½km NE along the A83 road to the foot of Glen Shira at 112103, then up the private road in the glen to the Lochan Shira dam. Continue along the road on the N side of the reservoir and over the col to the head of Glen Fyne. Go E down the Allt nan Taillir and up the Allt Coir' an Longairt to reach the road in Gleann nan Caorann. Follow this road down to Glenfalloch Farm.

100 Inveraman to Dalmally
24km/15mls   *Maps: OS 50/53;* **4**
   From Glenfalloch Farm, 1½km N of Inverarnan, a private Hydro Electric road goes WNW up Gleann nan Caorann on the S side of the Dubh Eas. When the road ends, continue up the Allt a' Mhinn to the pass between Meall nan Tighearn and Beinn a' Chleibh, then

down the Allt a' Chaorainn to Succoth Lodge from which a private road goes down to join the A85 road 3km E of Dalmally.

The glen from the pass down to Succoth Lodge has been planted with conifers, but the route is quite possible if followed along the line of pylons on the N side of the Allt a' Chaorainn.

101 Furnace (Loch Fyne) to Durran (Loch Awe)
12km/7½mls   *Maps: OS 55/52; 4*

Start from the A83 road at Auchendrain (about 3km N of Furnace) and follow a minor road SW for 1km to the bridge over the Leacann Water. Go steeply up the zigzag track NW into the forest. Continue W out of the forest along a path to Loch Leacann, then NW past Loch Airigh na Craige to re-enter the forest and join another road. Follow it NW on the NE side of the Abhainn a' Bhealaich to reach the B840 road a few hundred metres NE of Durran.

102 Furnace to Ford (Loch Awe)
20km/12½mls   *Maps: OS 55/52; 4*

Start from the A83 road 2km N of Furnace (or at Auchendrain 1km further N). Follow a private road past Brenachoille and WSW through the forest, beyond which a rough track continues to the derelict cottage at Carron. From there go NW uphill, steeply at first, along a track which in places is very rough and washed out. Pass several lochans on the undulating moorland and descend the track to reach the B840 near the SW end of Loch Awe, 2km E of Ford.

103 Furnace to Kilmichael Glassary
20km/12mls   *Maps: OS 55/52; 4*

Go by route 102 to the derelict cottage at Carron. Continue SW along a path into the forest where a forest road is joined about 300 metres E of Meall Reamhar. Continue SW along this road to Lechuary and the minor public road which leads to Kilmichael Glassary.

Routes 102 and 103 are shown on Roy's map of 1755. In droving times Kilmichael Glassary was a tryst for drovers coming from Islay, Jura and south-west Argyll, and route 103 was a drove road.

104 Dalavich to Oban
24km/15mls   *Maps: OS 49,55/52; **4***

Dalavich on Loch Awe is reached by bus from Taynuilt or Oban. From Barnaline Lodge, 1½km N of Dalavich, take the road up the river to the N bank of Loch Avich. About 1½km along the loch, near Lochavich House, take the track going NNE by Loch na Sreinge (the Loch of Lorn), just beyond which is the Carn Chailein where MacCailean Mor was slain in 1294. 400 metres past there take care to keep left when the track goes uphill, and descend by the Allt Braglenmore to the N bank of Loch Scamadale.

Go along this loch for 1km, then go steeply uphill by a track above the Eas Ruadh and cross it where the slope becomes less steep. Keep NW, descending to the road at the head of Loch Feochan about 6½km S of Oban. The main road into Oban can be avoided by going up the River Nell to Loch Nell and into Oban by Glen Cruitten.

An alternative from Loch Scamadale is to go down the glen by road to join the Oban road (A816) 3km S of Kilninver and 14½km S. of Oban.

Note: The section of the route from Loch Scamadale to Loch Feochan has been planted with conifers and part of it is difficult to find.

105 Kilchrenan to Oban
27km/17mls   *Maps: OS 49,50/52; **4***

Kilchrenan can be reached by bus from Taynuilt. From there go W up a burn to a wood and through it to a col, the Bealach Mor (240m). Descend on its W side to the S end of Loch Nant, enlarged as a reservoir and now covering part of the original track. Go S to the head of the loch, cross the Abhainn Cam Linne and continue up its N bank to Sior Loch. 1½km beyond the head of this loch go W to reach a rough road which leads down Glen Feochan to Kilmore on the A816 road 5km S of Oban. Instead of following this road, it is better to go along the much quieter road past Loch Nell and reach Oban by Glen Cruitten as in route 104.

SECTION 9
Loch Lomond to Loch Tay

106 Queenzieburn to Kippen
25km/15¹/₂mls   *Maps: OS 57,64/50,60; 5*

Go N from Queenzieburn by road uphill to Corrie. Beyond there a well-used track continues up to the Birkenburn Reservoir. Cross the dam and continue N alongside a fence for about 180 metres until it meets another fence at right angles. Go W along this for about 275 metres to a third fence going N, and follow this down to the edge of the mature forest at 674814, where a stile gives access to the forest road down to Burnhouse. From there take the forest road NW along the S side of the Carron Valley Reservoir to the dam at its W end.

Go E on the B818 road for 200 metres, then NE by road through the forest for 1km. There, at 684865, turn N to Cringate (ruin) and continue NW up the Endrick Water keeping to high ground (no real track) to Burnfoot (burn there difficult in spate). Then follow a faint track for 1¹/₂km to to reach a track which continues past the Spout of Ballochleam (waterfall) to Ballochleam farm, from where Kippen is reached *via* Dasher.

Routes 107 to 109 are in the Queen Elizabeth Forest Park and are more fully described, with map, in the Park Guide (HMSO).

107 Drymen to Aberfoyle
16km/10mls   *Maps: OS 57/54; 5*

Go N from Drymen by the old Gartmore road, climbing gradually to Bat a' Charchel (229m), then in another 2km (just before Drymen Road Cottage), turn left into the Queen Elizabeth Forest Park. Coloured signs mark the way from there through the forest to Aberfoyle, turning NE at 496984. An alternative starting point is Auchentroig – see route 108.

108 Drymen to Kinlochard
21km/13mls or 17¹/₂km/11mls   *Maps: OS 57/54; 5*
   From Drymen follow route 107 to the Queen Elizabeth Forest
Park, or take the Aberfoyle bus or go by car to Auchentroig Old
Schoolhouse (534926) on the main A81 road and from there go W
by the road past Hoish to join route 107 at 505936 (where there is
parking). The way onwards is marked by coloured signs. It leaves
route 107 at 496984 and goes W, crosses the Duchray Water and
comes out on Loch Ard near Couligartan, then goes W round the
head of the loch to Kinlochard.

109 Aberfoyle to Rowardennan
19km/12mls   *Maps: OS 56,57/53,54; 5*
   (a) Cross the River Forth to Kirkton and in 200 metres fork right,
passing Lochan Spling and Duchray Castle to join route 108 at
466992. Continue NW for 2km and at 453004 leave route 108,
turning W at the aqueduct, and go NW up the Duchray Water for
2km. At 429013 fork left and continue for about 600 metres to cross
a bridge over the Duchray Water. Go uphill beside the Bruach
Caorainn Burn to the ridge, where the Ben Lomond path from
Rowardennan is joined for the final 2¹/₂km down to Loch Lomond.
The summit of Ben Lomond (974m) is about 3km N up the ridge.
   (b) For a slightly shorter route, go W by road from Aberfoyle for
2km to Milton, turn left and after crossing the River Forth bear W on
the S of Loch Ard (following the higher of the two forest roads) to
Couligartan. Just beyond there join route 108, turn left (S) and in
about 400 metres turn right on joining route (a) above at 453004.
   The walking distance can be further shortened by starting from
Kinlochard and going S round the head of Loch Ard to join (b) near
Couligartan. Coloured signs (blue for Rowardennan) make it easy to
follow these routes.

110 Rowardennan to Inversnaid and Inverarnan
12km/7¹/₂mls and 23km/14¹/₂mls   *Maps: OS 56/53, 5*
   Rowardennan can be reached by road *via* Balmaha, or by ferry
from Inverbeg (April to September). From there a private road goes

N to Ptarmigan Lodge. Continue past it by a forest road for 4½km to its end and onwards by footpath past Cailness to Inversnaid Hotel. From there it may be possible to cross Loch Lomond by private ferry to Inveruglas, and there is a Postbus service to Aberfoyle.

The path continues N past Rob Roy's Cave and onwards by the well-defined, but in places very eroded and muddy path past Doune and Ardleish to Beinglas Farm. There cross the River Falloch to reach the A82 road 400 metres N of Inverarnan.

Note: This route follows the West Highland Way.

111 Aberfoyle to Callander

12km/7½mls   *Maps: OS 57/54; 5*

Leave the A81 road at the east end of Aberfoyle golf course, 2km E of the village. Go NE uphill through the forest by a track for 2½km to the NE edge of the forest. A well trodden track follows for about 1½km. Cross an open valley on the SE slope of the Menteith Hills to re-enter the forest and thereafter keep NE through a low pass until near West Dullater on the S side of Loch Venachar, from where it is 6km by road to Callander.

112 Callander to The Trossachs

18km/11mls   *Maps: OS 57/54; 5*

Cross the River Teith, and turn W along the road to the Water Works. Go along the S side of Loch Venachar until 2km beyond West Dullater, then go uphill round the S side of Invertrossachs to Culnagreine and the path leading W. Skirting the N end of Loch Drunkie, go W by forest roads to the E end of Loch Achray and follow the path along the S side of this loch.

At the Loch Achray Hotel take the forest road W, and keep straight ahead to the sluices at the outflow of Loch Katrine. Cross the Achray Water and return by road to the A821 ½km from the E end of Loch Katrine.

Alternatively, 2km beyond Loch Drunkie, go N across the Black Water by the bridge at 533064 and then E by road to Brig o'Turk, where the S end of route 115 is joined.

113 Kinlochard to The Trossachs by Ben Venue
10km/6mls   *Maps: OS 57/54; 5*

From Ledard, on the N side of Loch Ard, go up the path beside the Ledard Burn, at first on the W side, then on the E. When nearing Beinn Bhreac, continue NE along the path on the NW slope of Creag a' Bhealaich, across a col and then, still following a path, up to the NW top of Ben Venue (729m). Continue along a path which leads to the lower SE top.

From there either descend steeply NE to the Loch Katrine sluices and the road to the Loch Achray Hotel, or descend more easily S to the point where a path enters the Achray Forest, and follow this path (usually very wet and muddy) down Gleann Riabhach to a forest road and the Loch Achray Hotel.

It is possible as an easier variation of this route, omitting the summit of Ben Venue, to descend a path from the col between Creag a' Bhealaich and Ben Venue SE into the head of Gleann Riabhach, and go down this glen as described above.

114 Loch Katrine (Stronachlachar or The Trossachs) to Inverarnan
13km/8mls   *Maps: OS 56,57/53,54; 5*

(a) From Stronachlachar, which may be reached by Postbus from Aberfoyle, go NW along the private road on the S shore of Loch Katrine to its W end. From there follow the rough track up Glen Gyle below a line of electricity pylons for 3km and continue beyond the end of the track for a further 2km on the NE side of Glengyle Water (indistinct path) to the col at the head of the glen. Descend NW down a wide boggy corrie to cross the Ben Glas Burn and reach the path on its N side. Follow this path down to Beinglas Farm and cross the River Falloch to reach the A82 road 400 metres N of Inverarnan, 3km N of Ardlui.

(b) From The Trossachs this route may be started from the E end of Loch Katrine by taking the steamer *Sir Walter Scott* (during summer months only) to Stronachlachar and continuing as above. Alternatively, walk along the private road on the N shore of Loch Katrine to its W end and continue as in (a), in which case the total distance is 25km/15½mls.

115 The Trossachs (Brig o' Turk) to Balquhidder or Strathyre
16km/10mls   *Maps: OS 57/54; 5*
From Brig o'Turk go N along the road on the E side of the Glen
Finglas Reservoir and up Gleann nam Meann to 517148 where the
road turns W. From there go NE at first for about 300 metres on a
faint grassy path to a gate in a fence. Continue down the path
descending N to Gleann Dubh and and then E to Ballimore. From
there the road down Glen Buckie leads to Balquhidder.

To reach Strathyre, go E from Ballimore to Immeroin, climb
grassy slopes (very faint path) over the S shoulder of Beinn an
t-Sithein (gate in deer fence) and finally go down a waymarked path
through the forest to Strathyre.

116 Inverlochlarig to Inverarnan
15km/9¹/₂mls   *Maps: OS 56,57/53,54; 5*
This is the old coffin route from Glen Falloch to Balquhidder, as
the name of the pass Bealach nan Corp *(pass of the corpses)*
indicates. One can start by walking an additional 10km/6mls from
Balquhidder along the narrow public road on the N side of Loch
Voil and Loch Doine to the car park at its end, ¹/₂km E of
Inverlochlarig farm. (The site of the house where Rob Roy died).

Continue up the glen past the farm on a good track for 5km.
Beyond its end continue for 2km beside the headwaters of the River
Larig and make a rising traverse on the S side of the river to the
Bealach nan Corp at 360160. This col is broad and boggy and may
be confusing in mist.

Bear W to pass through a fence at the foot of Sidhean a' Chatha,
then go NW on a slightly descending traverse across the grassy SW
flank of Parlan Hill to reach the col at the head of Glen Gyle where
there is a small lochan. Descend NW down a wide boggy corrie to
cross the Ben Glas Burn and reach the path on its N side. Follow
this down to Beinglas Farm and the A82 road in Glen Falloch 400
metres N of Inverarnan.

It is equally possible to follow the River Larig to its source at the
col between Parlan Hill and Beinn Chabhair, cross this col and
descend to Lochan Beinn Chabhair and the start of the path down
to Beinglas Farm.

117 Balquhidder to Crianlarich
22km/14mls   *Maps: OS 51,56,57/57,54; 5*

Follow the road W from Balquhidder to Inverlochlarig where the
walk may be started at the car park at the end of the public road (see
route 116). Go N up the Inverlochlarig Glen and through the pass
between Stob Garbh and Stob Binnein. Continue down the
Benmore Glen, below the W slopes of Ben More, to the main road
150 metres E of Benmore Farm and 3km E of Crianlarich.

*Note: There are bulldozed roads up the Inverlochlarig Glen and
down the Benmore Glen. Apart from 3km at the summit of the pass,
the entire route from Inverlochlarig to Benmore Farm (9km/5^1/$_2$mls)
is on these roads.*

118 Balquhidder to Killin by Lulb
17km/10^1/$_2$mls   *Maps: OS 51/54; 5*

From Balquhidder Church go N up the road through the forest,
then a path beyond it on the E side of the Kirkton Glen to Lochan
an Eireannaich (600m). Continue down the E side of the Ledcharrie
Burn (no path) to the A85 road 1km E of Luib. (This is shown as a
road on Roy's map of 1755 and named 'Lairig Earne'). To reach
Killin, go E along the A85 for about 180 metres, then cross the River
Dochart and continue down its N side by the minor road to Killin.

119 Loch Lubnaig (Ardchullarie) to Lochearnhead
12km/8mls   *Maps: OS 51,57/54; 5*

Ardchullarie More is on Loch Lubnaig, 10km N of Callander on
the A84 road, and 5km S of Strathyre. On the N side of the house a
path climbs steeply to join a forest road which goes N up a glen. In
2km the watershed is reached and it is then 7km down Glen Ample,
below the W slopes of Stuc a' Chroin. Do not go through the farm
at Glenample, but follow the right of way on the W side of the Burn
of Ample at that point to reach the road leading down to the Falls
of Edinample, 2^1/$_2$km by road from Lochearnhead.

120 Callander to Lochearnhead
24km/15mls   *Maps: OS 51,57/54; 5*

From Callander take the road signposted to the Bracklinn Falls to
its end at Braeleny Farm. Continue N along the track to

Arivurichardich and climb the indistinct path rising across the W slope of Meall Odhar and over Meall na h-Iolaire into Gleann an Dubh Choirein. Descend NE to the junction of streams in this glen at the ruined bothy of Dubh Choirein.

From there go N up the deep glen between Ben Vorlich and Meall na Fearna , cross the pass at about 590m and descend Glen Vorlich. The path improves and eventually a track leads down the W side of the burn to Ardvorlich. From there it is 6km by road to Lochearnhead.

The amount of climbing can be reduced, and the distance increased by about 4km, by going E from Arivurichardich along a track to the bridge over the Allt an Dubh Choirein, and then following the path up the NE side of this stream to Dubh Choirein.

121 Callander to Comrie by Glen Artney
24km/15mls   *Maps: OS 57/54; 5*
Go by route 120 to the footbridge at 642130 near Arivuri-chardich. Then go E along the track below Meall Odhar and Tom Odhar to the crossing of the Allt an Dubh Choirein , and in another 2km reach the bridge over the Water of Ruchill. From there a road goes down the S side of Glen Artney to Comrie. Walkers should go to Auchinner and follow the path on the N bank of the river, which gives a much more pleasant walk.

"Lone Glen Artney's hazel shade" figures in Sir Walter Scott's *Lady of the Lake*. This route is shown as a road on Stobie's 1783 map of Perthshire.

122 Comrie to Ardeonaig (Loch Tay)
21km/13mls   *Maps: OS 51/54,48; 5*
Go NW up Glen Lednock by the road past Invergeldie and cross the bridge at 732279 to continue by the path and road on the S side of Loch Lednock Reservoir. Go round the head of the reservoir and back on the other side for about 800 metres to find the indistinct old track which climbs NW up the hillside, over the SW shoulder of Creag Uchdag and down to the col between Ruadh Mheall and Creag Uchdag. From there descend by the path down the Finglen Burn to Ardeonaig on Loch Tay.

123 Comrie to Ardtalnaig (Loch Tay)
24km/15mls   *Maps: OS 51/54,48; 5*
Follow route 122 for 8km to Invergeldie, then go NNE by the track up the west bank of the Invergeldie Burn, keeping to the west fork of this track up to the watershed (633m) NW of Ben Chonzie. Descend NW to Dunan near the head of Glen Almond and go N by a rough road down Gleann a' Chilleine to Ardtalnaig.

124 Newton Bridge (Amulree) to Ardtalnaig (Loch Tay)
25km/16mls   *Maps: OS 52/48; 5*
Newton Bridge is on the A822 road in the Sma' Glen, 13km NE of Crieff and 5½km S of Amulree. From there a private road and then a track go W up Glen Almond on the N bank of the River Almond for about 19km to Dunan just beyond the junction with route 123, which is followed to Ardtalnaig.

125 Newton Bridge to Aberfeldy by the Wade Road
24km/15mls   *Maps: OS 52/48; 5*
The starting point is the same as for route 124. The first 10 or 11km are easily followed, but the next part is on rather boggy ground, and the last section is the same as the present busy main road. It is recorded for its historic interest.
From Newton Bridge go N along the A822 road and in another 400 metres take the Old Wade Road on the left, which runs parallel to the main road. In another 2km the main road is joined, then in 800 metres the old road passes above Corrymuckloch and goes direct to Amulree. At Amulree the Wade Road climbs the hill and goes over Glen Fender to Glen Cochill, crosses and recrosses the A826 road to Aberfeldy and keeps up the W bank of the Cochill Burn for over 3km, but it is difficult to follow in many places, joining the A826 about 800 metres S of Loch na Craige, where forestry work has obliterated part of the Wade Road. Beyond the loch the Wade Road takes a fairly direct line close to the A826 downhill to Aberfeldy.
Another section of the Wade Road can be traced S of Newton Bridge. It leaves the A822 road opposite Foulford Inn 7km from Crieff and rejoins it at the start of the Sma' Glen.

126 Harrietfield (Glenalmond) to Kenmore

30¹/₂km/19mls   *Maps: OS 52/48,49,55; 5*

Harrietfield on the River Almond is reached by bus from Methven, or by road to Trinity College, then by the back avenue of the college to a footbridge over the Almond. From Harrietfield go W along the road for 1¹/₂km, then turn N by road up to Logiealmond Lodge, past it to the old quarry, then by track NW to Girron and Amulree. (The original right of way left Glenalmond at Frenchton, and went N by the Shelligan Burn to join route 126 at 942318).

From Amulree take the road up the N bank of the River Quaich and Loch Freuchie and on by Tirchardie to join the road over the Lairig Mile Marcachd to Kenmore. Lairig Mile Marcachd – *the pass of the mile of riding* – so named because of the level part on the summit.

The second part of this route is a very old road; it is mentioned in the *Chronicle of Fortingall* and is shown on Stobie's 1783 map of Perthshire, as well as on Roy's map of 1755.

127 Luncarty to Amulree or Dunkeld

24km/15mls   *Maps: OS 52/49; **5,6***

Cross the A9 road 1km N of Luncarty (8km from Perth) and go W along the Pitlandie road for about 500 metres to 085306. There turn right and go NW by an overgrown track to a well-defined track (at 084312) to Gellybanks. Then go W and continue by a farm road to Cowford Cottage. From there a track is well defined to Gourdiehill. Continue NW by a minor road to Little Glenshee and up Glen Shee to Rosecraig, then NW down into Strath Braan at Ballachraggan. From there it is 5km W to Amulree.

Alternatively, to reach Dunkeld, go E by the A822 road for 5km to Trochry, then cross the River Braan and go down the N bank along the Old Military Road and through The Hermitage.

SECTION 10
The Ochils, Lomonds and Sidlaws

128 Tillicoultry to Blackford or Gleneagles
14¹/₂km/9mls   *Maps: OS 58/55;* **5**

Go up the path on the E side of Mill Glen and above the Gannel Burn to the pass on the NW of King's Seat Hill. Then turn NW over the pass (570m), skirting W of Skythorn Hill (path indistinct) and down the Broich Burn (high above its east bank) to Backhills on the Upper Glendevon Reservoir. From that point there are two possible routes, depending on one's destination.

(a) For Blackford go to the left round the head of the reservoir, cross the River Devon and go NW up Glen Bee and down the Glen of Kinpauch (or over Kinpauch Hill) to Kinpauch and Blackford.

(b) For Gleneagles go to the right at Backhills and along the reservoir road past the Lower Glendevon Reservoir. Just before the A823 Glen Devon road is reached, take a track on the left which is an old road going at first alongside the modern road and then down the W side of Glen Eagles to the A9 road 2¹/₂km from Blackford.

129 Dollar to Auchterarder
19km/12mls   *Maps: OS 58/55;* **5**

From Dollar go up by Castle Campbell and the E side of the Burn of Care and NE by the Maiden's Well to Glenquey Reservoir. Cross the River Devon near Burnfoot, and continue up the Borland Glen, and N by the Coul Burn to Coulshill. Finally go 4¹/₂km by a minor road to Upper Cloan and Auchterarder.

130 Glenfarg to Bridge of Earn
10km/6mls   *Maps: OS 58/55;* **6**

Take the B996 road N from Glenfarg for 800 metres, forking left at the signpost to 'Wicks of Baigley' almost due N, and in another 1km turn left off this route to Lochelbank and continue NNW over

Dron Hill by the 'Wallace Road' to West Dron. Finally go N to the school at Bridge of Earn.

This is part of the old road to Perth shown on Roy's map of 1755 and referred to by Scott in the first chapter of *The Fair Maid of Perth*, where he says that the summit of it is "one of the most beautiful points of view in Britain".

131 Lomond Hills – Falkland to Kinnesswood

14¹/₂km/9mls   *Maps: OS 58/55;* **6**

From Falkland go S steeply up through woods towards East Lomond, or from a point 2km SE of Falkland on the A912 road go uphill by the marked side road to the relay station and car park on Purin Hill. By either route reach the top of East Lomond (424m). Descend W to Craigmead carpark (at 227063) and continue WNW along a good track over Balharvie Moss to the short steep climb to West Lomond (522m). Descend SW to Glen Vale (also called the Covenanters' Glen) where there are interesting caves, one of which is known as John Knox's Pulpit. Continue down a path to Glenlomond, and reach Kinnesswood along the A911 road 2km further S.

132 Bridgefoot (Dundee) to Glamis

14km/8¹/₂mls   *Maps: OS 54,50;* **6**

From Bridgefoot (6km NW of Dundee) go N by the public road to South Balluderon and up Balluderon Hill. Continue in the same direction through a gap (345m) between Craigowl Hill and Auchterhouse Hill, the highest points in the Sidlaws, to reach Wester Denoon. From there a public road descends by Slaughs to Glamis.

133 Longforgan to Newtyle

19¹/₂km/12mls   *Maps: OS 53/49;* **6**

From Longforgan go by the public road NW to Dron, then by Redmyre Loch to Balshando Hill. Continue NE by Balshando and Lundie to reach Wester Keith and Long Loch, then, keeping Newtyle Hill on the left, finish the walk to Newtyle.

SECTION 11
Tay, Tummel, Glen Lyon and Rannoch

134 Pitlochry to Grandtully
8km/5mls   *Maps: OS 52/48,49; 5*
   Cross the River Tummel by the footbridge to Port-na-Craig. Go
SW uphill by Middleton of Fonab and a zigzag track through the
forest, over the ridge and down to the Tullypowrie Burn. Finally go
down the burn by a path past Tullypowrie to Grandtully.

135 Blair Atholl to Loch Tummel
11½km/7mls   *Maps: OS 52/48; 5*
   Cross the River Garry at Blair Atholl and go 3km up the river to
Balnansteuartach at the foot of the Allt Bhaic, then SW uphill to the
W side of Loch Bhac, and south over the hill to Tressait and the Loch
Tummel Hotel.
   This route is shown as a road on Stobie's map of Perthshire in
1783, and on a map of 1725 (in the British Library) as part of the
'road' between Inversnaid Barracks and Ruthven Barracks at
Kingussie. The route from Inversnaid was by Stronachlachar, the
head of Loch Katrine, the N side of Loch Voil, Balquhidder,
Lochearnhead, NE to Loch Tay and Kenmore, the W end of Loch
Tummel, Blair Atholl, thence N by the Minigaig Pass.
   An alternative parallel route to the E end of Loch Tummel can be
taken. After crossing the River Garry, go due S ascending by a zigzag
path through open woodland to reach Tomanraid (362m). At
865629 turn left to descend *via* Fincastle Farm and Glen Fincastle
to Loch Tummel.

136 Calvine to Loch Tummel
9km/5½mls   *Maps: OS 43,52/48; 5*
   Cross the River Garry to Old Struan church and continue E over
Errochty Water for 700 metres to the SRWS signpost at 816654.

Proceed S over a field to a gate and uphill through birchwood to a forestry gate (at 810646) and ladder stile. Follow the forest track SSE to exit from the plantation at 815635 over a ladder stile. (Avoid following the bulldozed track which stays within the forest). Continue S over shoulder for 1½km to ladder stile (816625) and into older forest W of Loch Bhac, then due S to exit *via* gate (815608) and down to the Loch Tummel Hotel.

137 Fortingall to Kinloch Rannoch
17½km/11mls   *Maps: OS 51/48; 5*
    From Fortingall take the track up the spur E of the Allt Odhar, climbing NNE for 1½km then NW for 2½km to reach the col between Meall nan Eun and Meall Crumach (fine views of Schiehallion). Continue NW over a spur to descend to Glenmore Bothy in the glen ahead. From there go NW to cross the Allt Creag a' Mhadaidh to Uamh Tom a' Mhor-fhir (old sheilings), where Gleann Mor divides in two. Then go up the NW branch of the glen and N over the saddle to the W of Schiehallion to the Tempar Burn and down the track on the E side of this burn to the road, 3km E of Kinloch Rannoch.

138 Innerwick to Kinloch Rannoch
16km/10mls   *Maps: OS 51/48; 5*
    From the church at Innerwick in Glen Lyon (1½km E of Bridge of Balgie) follow the track NW up the E side of the burn, then, in 1½km, turn NNE to the Lairig Ghallabhaich (478m) (also known as the Kirk Road) and continue down along the Allt Droilichean and into the forest until the stream turns NE. At that point there is a choice:
    (a) NE down the Allt na Bogair to Carie on Loch Rannoch, 5km from Kinloch Rannoch,
    (b) by the left fork of the track N through the Black Wood of Rannoch down to Dall (Rannoch School) on Loch Rannoch.
    The route from Innerwick to Dall is shown as a road on Stobie's 1783 map of Perthshire. It is part of an old drove road and those prepared to add 19km to the walk can start along this old route from Killin, by road up Glen Lochay for 5km to Duncroisk, then NE up

the Allt Dhuin Croisg (path for some distance but rather wet) to the pass, the Lairig Breisleich. About 3km beyond the pass the road between Loch Tay and Glen Lyon is joined about 3km from Bridge of Balgie.

139 Innerwick to Loch Rannoch
13km/8mls   *Maps: OS 51/48;* **5**

For the first 800 metres from Innerwick the route is the same as 138. Then instead of turning up the Allt Ghallabhaich, cross this stream and go NW up an intermittent track to the Lairig a' Mhuic (*pass of swine*), and over the S shoulder of Meall nan Sac to reach the Dall Burn. Continue by the track NW to the Allt Camghouran and down this stream to Loch Rannoch. From the point where the road is reached, it is 14km W to Rannoch Station or 12km E to Kinloch Rannoch.

140 Killin to Bridge of Orchy or Tyndrum by Loch Lyon
40km/25mls   *Maps: OS 50,51/47,48;* **4,5**

Go by the public road up Glen Lochay to Kenknock, then by the private Hydro Electric road NW over the pass to the dam at the E end of Loch Lyon. (The dam can also be reached by public road up Glen Lyon from Aberfeldy, and there is a Postbus service between Aberfeldy and Lubreoch at the dam.)

Keep to the N side of Loch Lyon (path for about 5km, then rough going) to the W end of the loch. Continue W over the pass between Beinn Mhanach and Beinn nam Fuaran and go down the Allt a' Chuirn to the ruined house at Ais-an t-Sidhein, where the Gaelic poet Duncan Ban MacIntyre once lived. Continue along the track beside the Allt Kinglass down the Auch Gleann and under the great viaduct of the West Highland Railway.

Just before reaching Auch, turn NW and follow the track, which at this point is the West Highland Way, beside the railway to Bridge of Orchy. Alternatively, turn S and follow the West Highland Way (which at this point is also a right of way) for 5km to Tyndrum.

An alternative route to avoid the the last part of the difficult N shore of Loch Lyon beyond Gleann Meran is to head up Gleann Cailliche to the col between Beinn a' Chuirn and Beinn Achaladair and from there go down to Ais-an t Sidhein.

141 Bridge of Orchy to Loch Rannoch
28km/17mls   *Maps: OS 50,51/47; 4,5*

This was once an important drove road, but today it includes a section through maturing forest which may frustrate the walker.

For the first 1½km the old drove road coincides with the new A82, and for the next 1½km it is closer to the railway. Both roads unite again as far as the NE corner of Loch Tulla where the drove road, now a farm track, goes NE to Achallader Farm. After 2km the track crosses to the NW bank of the Water of Tulla at Barravourich (ruin) and continues up the NW bank for 5km to Gorton bothy.

About 2½km beyond Gorton the route goes under the railway (alongside the Water of Tulla and close to the Madagan Moineach, a mossy place which was a drove stance) and from there continues for about 1km NE into forest. Entry is best effected by seeking a gated section near a small windmill (which provides current for the electrified fence). Once through the fence it is better to follow the long forest ride (the original route is now lost) and continue NE for 7km to emerge near the ruin at Lochan Dubh Grunnd nan Darachan (470540). Continue by the track down the W side of Gleann Chomraidh to Bridge of Gaur at the W end of Loch Rannoch, 9km from Rannoch Station on the West Highland Railway.

From the railway crossing mentioned above, a strenuous round is possible by going S up the Allt Learg Mheuran, through a narrow pass to Gleann Meran and Loch Lyon, and back to Bridge of Orchy by route 140.

SECTION 12
Glen Coe and Appin

142 Tyndrum to Kingshouse Hotel and Glencoe village by the old road

30km/19mls and 47km/29mls   *Maps: OS 41,50/47;* **4**

There have been four stages in the history of the road across the Black Mount and through Glen Coe: (a) the original drove road, for centuries the main route from north-western Scotland to the Lowlands; (b) the Old Military Road, constructed about 1750, largely on the line of the original drove road, with occasional deviations; (c) the 19th-century road, also largely on the original line but deviating in considerable stretches from the military road so as to provide easier gradients; and (d) the present road, the A82. Very little of road (c) is now in use by vehicles, and it provides a fine route for walkers.

From Tyndrum go up the W bank of the Crom Allt for 1½km, then cross the West Highland Railway and continue close to it, first on one side and then the other, to Bridge of Orchy. There cross the River Orchy and go NW uphill through forest over the Mam Carraigh and down to Inveroran Hotel and Forest Lodge. Then go N along the foot of the great range of Black Mount peaks and corries to Ba Bridge and Kingshouse Hotel.

For the next 13km through Glen Coe the remaining sections of the old road are rather discontinuous, but there are still passable stretches that avoid the traffic on the A82 (see OS map). Finally, for the last 5km to Loch Leven, the old road from Clachaig Inn to Glencoe village gives a pleasant end to this long walk, the wooded glen being in marked contrast to the bare expanse of Rannoch Moor and the stark peaks of upper Glen Coe.

From Tyndrum to Altnafeadh this route coincides with the West Highland Way.

143 Rannoch Station to Kingshouse Hotel
19km/12mls   *Maps: OS 41,42/46,47;* **4,5**

From the station go W round the head of Loch Laidon, keeping to the loch shore and avoiding a forest road branching right after 400 metres. Continue for $2^{1}/_{2}$km along the NW shore, then climb gradually until about 60m above the loch and contour across the hillside at about this level until above the ruined cottage of Tigh na Cruaiche, about $6^{1}/_{2}$km from Rannoch Station.

From there strike due W away from the loch, first rising slightly, then descending again, and follow a track across several streams to reach Black Corries Lodge at the foot of Meall nan Ruadhag, from where there is a road for 5km to Kingshouse Hotel. Electricity pylons mark the line from Rannoch to Black Corries.

The middle section of this route is rather boggy in wet weather and it is advisable to attempt it only in dry clear weather.

144 Bridge of Orchy to Taynuilt
40km/25mls   *Maps: OS 50/46,47,53;* **4**

Take the old Glen Coe road (route 142) for 5km by Inveroran Hotel to Victoria Bridge, then go W by a track up the N bank of the Abhainn Shira. After passing the little climbers' hut at the foot of the Allt Toaig, do not take the road through the forest to Clashgour Farm as the right of way follows the bank of the river. 4km W of Victoria Bridge cross to the S bank by an old suspension bridge and continue W to Loch Dochard.

From there go SW over to Glen Kinglass and descend this glen (good track from Glen Kinglass Lodge onwards) to Ardmaddy on Loch Etive, 25km from Inveroran and 28km from Bridge of Orchy. From Ardmaddy the track continues along the lochside for 5km to Glennoe, whence a forest road leads to Bridge of Awe, 3km by road from Taynuilt.

From Acharn, about halfway down Glen Kinglass, the route over the Lairig Dhoireann (610m) and down Glen Strae to Dalmally is about $6^{1}/_{2}$km shorter than going to Taynuilt – see route 145.

145 Dalmally to Glen Coe
48km/30mls   *Maps: OS 41,50/46,47,53;* **4**
Take the B8077 road to the bridge over the River Strae and go up the W side of Glen Strae, along a forestry road for about 1½km, then N uphill by the W side of a stream to the Lairig Dhoireann. Go downhill by the Allt Dhoireann for about 1km, then strike due W down the hillside to Acharn in Glen Kinglass, and descend this glen to Ardmaddy on Loch Etive. Follow the E bank of the loch N to Kinlochetive, the crossings of the Allt Ghiusachan and Allt Coire na Larach may be difficult in spate. Continue to Coiletir and the bridge over the River Etive just beyond there to join route 146 up Glen Etive.

146 Bonawe (Loch Etive) to Glen Goe
42km/26mls   *Maps: 41,50/46,47;* **4**
From Bonawe (reached by bus from Oban), follow the W side of Loch Etive by Craig and Cadderlie. 2km beyond Cadderlie bear N from the loch-shore track by a forestry road to reach the bridge over the Allt Easach between Dail and Barrs. Regain the lochside path and follow it to the head of Loch Etive. From there continue up Glen Etive by road to Dalness, from where there are three possibilities:

(a) continue by road up Glen Etive to Kingshouse Hotel;

(b) go due N by the path up to the Lairig Eilde, the pass on the W side of Buachaille Etive Beag, and down to the Glen Coe road about 5½km E of Clachaig Hotel and 7km from Glen Coe youth hostel;

(c) go NE through the Lairig Gartain to the Glen Coe road at Altnafeadh.

147 Loch Creran to Ballachulish
16km/10mls   *Maps: OS 41,50/46;* **4**
From the A828 road bridge at the head of Loch Creran, (reached by the Oban to Fort William bus) go NE up the Glen Creran road. About 6km up the glen, and after entering the forest, go uphill along

the forest road above Salachail. It turns N and goes to within 1km of the pass (410m). Beyond the pass the path is indistinct and drops steeply NNE down to Gleann an Fhiodh. Cross the River Laroch and follow a good path down its W bank to Ballachulish.

148 Kingshouse Hotel to Kinlochleven
14½km/9mls   *Maps: OS 41/47; 4*

This is a continuation of the Old Military Road described in route 142. The route leaves the A82 road 4km W of Kingshouse Hotel at Altnafeadh and climbs NW by the steep 'Devil's Staircase', a series of sharp bends reaching the pass at 550m. The old road then descends the hillside N then NW to join the access road from Kinlochleven to the Blackwater Reservoir, and follows this down to the village.

The Old Military Road to Kinlochleven was abandoned about 1785 when a new road was made through Glen Coe to the ferry at Ballachulish. For the continuation to Fort William, see route 223 on page 125.

This route is part of the West Highland Way

On the right of way west from Loch Tulla towards Glen Kinglass (route 144)

Looking south-west down Glen Tilt (route 177)

Approaching the Lairig Ghru from the south (route 181)

The Lairig Ghru from the edge of Rothiemurchus Forest (route 181)

SECTION 13
Mull

149 Salen – Loch Ba – Lochbuie
30km/19mls   *Maps: OS 48,49/45,51;* **10**
    From Salen follow the Loch na Keal road for 6km to Ba Bridge
and turn left along the private road on the S side of Loch Ba for 3km.
Climb up Glen Clachaig to the col (332m) 2½km due E of Ben
More, which can be climbed from there. From the col make a rising
traverse for 1km S over the shoulder of A'Chioch and descend to
Ardvergnish. Go round the head of Loch Scridain to Rossal Farm
and climb SSE beside the Allt Atharaidh, then NE to reach Lochan
Tana at the col between Beinn nam Feannag and Beinn na Croise.
Go E then SE round the head of Glen Byre and across the shoulder
of Beinn nan Gobhar, descending gradually to Lochbuie.

150 Lochbuie to Salen by Glen Forsa
24km/15mls   *Maps: OS 48,49/45,51;* **10**
    From Lochbuie go N up the E side of Gleann a' Chaiginn Mhoir
to the E bank of Loch Airdeglais. Beyond it cross the stream to the
W side of Loch an Ellen and climb up to the A849 road. Follow the
old road NE for 4km almost to the ruined house of Torness, then go
N over the low pass to Glen Forsa and down this glen by a forest
road to join the A849 2½km E of Salen.

151 Dervaig to Salen
19½km/12mls   *Maps: OS 47,48/45;* **10**
    From Dervaig go E along the Tobermory road for 2½km to
Achnadrish (8km from Tobermory). There follow a minor road and
track SE above the SW shore of Loch Frisa into a forest. Beyond the
forest continue along a path which climbs away from the loch round
the SW side of Cnoc nan Dubh Leitire and then descends gradually
to Tenga in Glen Aros. Finally go along the minor road down this
glen to join the A848 2km NW of Salen.

SECTION 14
The Eastern Grampians

152 Dunkeld to Kirkmichael by Lochan Oisinneach Mor
24km/15mls   *Maps: OS 52 or 53/49;* **6**
   Take the A923 Blairgowrie road for 180 metres to a signpost on the left marking the way N by Cally Loch and Birkenburn. In 3km, on reaching Mill Dam, turn right and follow the track on its E side, then NE below Deuchary Hill to Santa Crux Well, an inconspicuous spring beyond Grewshill.
   Continue N by the Buckny Burn and E of Lochan Oisinneach Mor to Lochan Oisinneach Beag. Go N from there past Creag Gharbh, then NE across the moor to the SW corner of a plantation. Go E along its S edge and cross two stiles into newly planted pine woods above Cultalonie. Descend NE down a wooded slope to reach a minor road leading to Kirkmichael.
   Alternatively, from Dowally (7km N from Dunkeld along the A9 road) go uphill to Raor Lodge, then NE to Loch Ordie and N from there to Lochan Oisinneach Mor to join the previous route. The route can also be joined from Ballinluig *via* Tulliemet.

153 Dunkeld to Kirkmichael by Loch Benachally
24km/15mls   *Maps: OS 52 or 53/49;* **6**
   Follow the A923 Blairgowrie road for 5½km to Butterstone, then go NNE by Leduckie to the SE end of Loch Benachally. Continue N over the moor and across the head of the Baden Burn to the W corner of Blackcraig Forest. From there descend to Loch Charles, go down a track to Woodhill Farm and cross the River Ardle to Ballintuim, 6km S of Kirkmichael.
   Having reached Woodhill Farm, instead of crossing the river to Ballintuim, it is possible to go up the W side of Strathardle past Dalnabreck, Pitcarmick, Dalvey and Cultalonie to reach Kirkmichael. Between Dalnabreck and Dalvey keep uphill above the hill dyke to avoid the policies of Pitcarmick.

154 Blairgowrie to Kirkmichael
22km/14mls   *Maps: OS 53/49;* **6**

From Kinloch, 3km W of Blairgowrie along the A923 road, go N to Middleton Farm. 1km further bear NW by the track across Cochrage Muir and in 3km enter Blackcraig Forest by the gate at 127497. Continue NW to Croft of Blackcraig, which can also be reached by a forest road going W from Bridge of Cally. Descend NW to Blackcraig and continue along the W side of Strathardle to Woodhill to join route 153. The continuation to Kirkmichael along Strathardle is described above.

155 Ballinluig to Kirkmichael
16km/10mls   *Maps: OS 52 or 53/49;* **6**

From Ballinluig go uphill by a minor road past Tulliemet House to reach a gate giving access to the open moor. Continue NNE by a track to within ½km of Loch Broom at 014573. At that point bear NE to go round the S corner of a deer fence along the forest boundary. Follow it NE on the N side of Sgorr Gorm (502m) and descend NE across The Back Burn to join a track 300 metres E of Mains of Glenderby. Continue along this track E through the forest and past chalets to reach Kirkmichael

156 Killiecrankie to Kirkmichael
26km/16mls   *Maps: OS 43/48,49;* **5,6**

Go NE by the private road up the W side of the Allt Girnaig and across the fields to Orchilmore. (This can also be reached from Aldclune by the road passing the site of the Battle of Killicrankie). Keep up the glen and cross the Girnaig by the footbridge 180 metres above the ford which is 800 metres S of Loinmarstaig. Beyond there the path swings round E to Reinakyllich, from where there is no track. Strike across rough ground to join route 157 (see below) about 1½km SE of Shinagag, and follow it to Kirkmichael

157 Blair Atholl to Kirkmichael
29km/10mls   *Maps: OS 43/48,49;* **5,6**

Go N from Blair Atholl to the Old Bridge of Tilt and Middlebridge, (signpost to Strathardle), then E to the N end of Loch Moraig, where the public road ends. Continue ENE on a private road (no vehicles) below the foot of Carn Liath (974m) and SE to

Shinagag. There strike SE across rough ground to the Allt na Leacainn Moire. Where this burn goes S through the gap on the E side of Creag Spardain, cross it and go SE over a low pass on the shoulder of the hill and descend to the road at Dalnavaid in Glen Brerachan. Follow the road E for 3km, then cross the River Ardle to reach the road to Kindrogan. Continue on the W side of the river, passing Dalreoch and Tullochcurran, to Kirkmichael. (This route is shown on Roy's map of 1755).

158 Kirkmichael to Glen Tilt and Blair Atholl
50km/31mls   *Maps: OS 43/41,48,49;* **5,6**
    Cross the River Ardle and go N to Dalreoch, recrossing to Enochdhu. Continue by road for 1½km, turning right and go N by Glenfernate Lodge up the Allt Fearnach for 7km to Daldhu. From there two routes are possible:
    (a) a shorter route goes up the Glen Loch Burn by track to Loch Loch, along the E side of the loch and then N down the An Lochain Burn to Glen Tilt. If the Tilt is too deep to ford to reach the path on its W bank, follow the E bank for 3km down to a bridge. Another 3km down Glen Tilt is Forest Lodge, from where a road runs down the glen for 13km to Blair Atholl.
    (b) a slightly longer route from Daldhu is to follow the private road N to Fealar Lodge, and then descend from the lodge to Glen Tilt, reaching it near the Falls of Tarf.

159 Kirkmichael to Spittal of Glenshee
14km/8½mls   *Maps: OS 43/49;* **6**
    Take route 158 to Enochdhu (signpost), then go NE by Dirnanean and Braegarrie to the foot of Elrig, and up the Allt Doire nan Eun to the pass on the N side of An Lairig. Finally, go NE down the Coire Lairige to Spittal of Glenshee. (Shown as a road on the map of 1755).

160 Kirkmichael to Glen Shee
8km/5mls   *Maps: OS 43/49;* **6**
    The original path beside the hotel is now impassable for about 300 metres, but opposite the telephone exchange go into the farm yard and turn right uphill into a field, soon to rejoin the original path on the right. Continue NE to Ashintully Castle and then past two

small lochs. Beyond these turn E over the Ennoch Burn and across the S slope of Lamh Dearg to Lair in Glen Shee. (From Lair a road goes E to Folda in Glen Isla, see route 162).

161 Alyth to Glen Shee and Kirkmichael
29km/18mls   *Maps: OS 43,53/49;* **6**
 Go NW round Alyth Hill by Whiteside, by road past Gauldswell to Tullymurdoch, then N by the track to Craighead. Continue N to the top of the Hill of Three Cairns, and then descend W to the Alyth Burn. Go up the burn and head NW straight over the moor to Blacklunans in Glen Shee. From there go S by road to Dalrulzion and then W by road to Kirkmichael.
 Alternatively, from Blacklunans go N for 3km to Clackavoid, cross the river to Lair and follow route 160 (in reverse) to Kirkmichael.

162 Glen Isla (Folda) to Glen Clova
26km/16mls   *Maps: OS 43,44/49,50;* **6**
 From Folda in Glen Isla go N for 800 metres by road until 100 metres short of the bridge, then NE up the hill track and over the ridge to the NE of Auchintaple Loch. The track descends into, but loses itself in, the moors around the Muckle Burn. Make for the 'glach' (pass) between Bada Crionard and Craigie Law; there is a stile where a path leads into the plantation. Go through the 'glach' and SE on the forestry road to Glenmarkie Lodge.
 From Glenmarkie Lodge go first E, then SE, and then NE through the Moss of Glanny, either by a track on the N side of the Moss or by the forest road on the S side, to Glenhead Lodge. Go NE through Drumshade Plantation (gates at both ends) and over Hill of Strone to Curmuir on the Glen Prosen road. Go down the glen for 2½km to Inchmill, and then NE by the E side of the Burn of Inchmill and over Drumwhern to Glen Clova near Eggie, 5km SE of Clova Inn.

163 Glen Isla to Glen Doll and Glen Clova
21km/13mls   *Maps: OS 44/41,49;* **6**
 Kirkton of Glenisla is reached by road from Alyth or, if walking, over the E side of the Hill of Alyth, then by Dykehead and Kilry, and N over Broom Hill.

From East Mill Farm, 800 metres E of Kirkton of Glenisla, go N by the forest road to Glenmarkie Lodge. From there two routes are possible:

(a) Go up Glen Finlet (forestry road part way) and at the head of the glen go NE over the pass into Glen Prosen and down to Kilbo (ruin), from where a faint track goes NE to the pass just S of the Shank of Drumfollow. Continue by the path down the Burn of Kilbo, crossing a deer fence (stile) into the Glen Doll Forest, and across the River South Esk to the road at the head of Glen Clova, 400 metres from Glen Doll youth hostel, and 6km from Clova Inn. For the continuation to Ballater see route 173.

(b) An alternative, about 8km longer, is to go E from Glenmarkie Lodge by route 162 to Cormuir in Glen Prosen. Turn up the glen, by road for 2½km, then by track for 5½km, to Kilbo. From there continue as above.

164 Clova to Tarfside
24km/15mls   *Maps: OS 44/42; 6*
From Clova go NE uphill, a steep climb of 4km passing on the S of Loch Brandy, to the top of Green Hill (865m). Continue E to the summit of White Hill, NE along the ridge over Muckle Cairn, and then descend steeply to Inchgrundle, from where a road goes alongside Loch Lee to Invermark (where route 172 goes left to Ballater), and E to Tarfside (see route 170).

165 Noranside (Tannadice) to Tarfside
26km/16mls   *Maps: OS 44/42,50; 6*
From Noranside (3km N of Tannadice) go E along the Edzell road to Fern and Balquharn. Take the road NW to Afflochie and up the E side of Cruick Water for 500 metres. Proceed NW on a track round to the W shoulder of Hill of Mondurran and then NE to Waterhead on the Water of Saughs. Go down Glen Lethnot for 3km to Tillybardine and follow the signposted track through the Clash of Wirren to Tarfside *via* East Knock and Cowie Hill.

The Mounth Paths
The long range of hills between Deeside and the Glens of Angus, extending for some 80km, has been known from early times as the

Mounth, and this name has come to be applied to the old rights of way which cross the hills. The following list of Mounth passes prepared in the 17th century by Sir James Balfour of Denmilne (1600-1651) is printed in the Spalding Club Collections on the Shires of Aberdeen and Banff, published in 1843:

1. Causey or Cowie Mounth. This is the old road from Aberdeen to the south, mentioned in writings from the 14th century onwards. It leaves the South Deeside road 1km from the (old) Bridge of Dee and is still in use by motor vehicles as far as Causeyport. The District Council has embarked on a scheme to open the onward route to Muchalls for pedestrians and persons on horseback and cycles.
    2. Elsick Mounth (route 166).
    3. Cryne Corse Mounth (route 167).
    4. Stock Mounth (route 168).
    5. Builg Mounth (route 169).
    6. Cairn a' Mount (public road).
    7. Forest of Birse Mounth (route 170).
    8. Mounth Gammel or Fir Mounth (route 171).
    9. Mount Keen (route 172).
  10. Capel Mounth (route 173).
  11. Cairnwell (public road).

Balfour does not mention the Tolmounth (route 175), nor the Monega Pass (route 176). The Mounth paths are more fully described in the Scottish Mountaineering Club's guide *The Cairngorms* (1992) by Adam Watson, and also in G.M.Fraser's *The Old Deeside Road* (1921).

166 Drumoak to Stonehaven (The Elsick Mounth)
19km/12mls   *Maps: OS 45/40,43; 7*
    At Drumoak, 18km W of Aberdeen, turn SE to cross the Dee at Park Bridge, then go S by Durris House, Denside and West Brachmont to the Y-junction at 807045. From there a forest road leads S for some 400 metres until another forest road leads E,S and SE to emerge from the forest NE of Bawdy Craig.
    This is not the original route, which enters the forest about 100 metres beyond the last mentioned forest road and goes S through

Strathgyle Wood to reach the forest boundary SW of Bawdy Craig. It is not easy to follow because of recent (1994) forestry operations.

The route then goes S over a spur to Easter Auquhollie and from there SE past Nether Auquhollie to join the Slug Road (A957) at Mowtie, 5km from Stonehaven.Balfour (see note above) describes the Elsick Mounth as going from Stonehaven to Drum.

This route by Auquhollie is the only route from Stonehaven to Deeside shown on Garden's map of Kincardine in 1776. One branch by Denside went to the old ford on the River Dee at Tilbouries, 1½km S of Drum. It is also shown on Roy's map of 1755. Above Mowtie is the site of the Roman camp at Raedykes.

167 Banchory to Glenbervie (Cryne Corse Mounth)
21½km/13½mls   *Maps: OS 45/40,43; 7*
From Banchory cross the Bridge of Feugh, take the road upstream and at the first fork go left to join in 5km the Slug Road (A957) at Blairydryne. Proceed along it to the sharp bend beyond Spyhill Farm and from there go S up the minor road towards the TV station. Some 250 metres before reaching it turn SE off this road to shortly meet a line of electricity pylons which follow the Cryne Corse Mounth for the most part to the main track along the Cowie Water.

Follow this SW for a short distance before turning left across a bridge over the Cowie Water by a forest road (signposted as a mountain bicycle track) which leads uphill passing a large gravel pit on the left. Keep straight on at the immediately following junction and aim SE for the road at Hill of Quithel (774856). This descends to the road to Stonehaven. Turn right there to the former schoolhouse (at 757837) and then go left by Goosecruives to Glenbervie and again left to Drumlithie.

168 Strachan to Glenbervie (The Stock Mounth)
19km/12mls   *Maps: OS 45/40,43; 7*
Take the B974 road S across the Water of Feugh for 400 metres to turn first left to Moss-side and about 300 metres further on take a farm track going S to a gate at Blarourie (700897). This gives entry to a forest road which goes SE between Shillofad and North Dennetys. The route then descends and crosses the Burn of

Sheeoch, skirts the W side of Monluth Hill and meets the main forest road on the N side of the Cowie Burn. Crossing the bridge over the burn, the walker may follow the main forest road S and SW to skirt the W side of Leachie Hill and descend past the site of Maxie Well to Chapelton Croft (736832). From there a farm track is followed past Chapelton Farm to the Stonehaven road and across it to Glenbervie. An alternative route from the Cowie Water by the E side of Leachie Hill is at present (1994) impassable because of afforestation and forestry operations.

169 Strachan to Auchenblae (The Builg Mounth)

20km/12½mls   *Maps: OS 45/40,43;* **7**

This is an ancient right of way from Strachan in Feughside to Paldy Fair, near Glenfarquhar Lodge N of Auchenblae.

Take the B974 road from Strachan as far as the Bridge of Bogendreip. Just before the new bridge over the Water of Dye take a main forest road leading sharply uphill to the SE. It soon leads in a generally S direction and goes through the forest for about 3½km. On leaving the forest the track is quite clear, curving round the base of Hare Hill to join a forest road below Little Kerloch. Leave it at about 683868 by a path heading SE along a forest ride towards the Builg Burn. Continue over rough ground to the pass between Tipperweir and The Builg where an old track leads into the forest. This is followed SW then SE along the West Burn of Builg. (Alternatively, where the old track in the forest turns SW a ride with a wall on its left-hand side, possibly the old track, may be followed SE to join the main track at East Burn of Builg). From the junction of the two burns continue the descent to Corsebauld and Chapelton Farm, from where a farm road going SW leads to the Stonehaven road, Mains of Glenfarquhar and Auchenblae.

Note: 'Builg Road, a Foot Path' is marked on Garden's map of 1776.

170 Aboyne to Tarfside and Edzell (The Fungle Road)

42km/26mls   *Maps: OS 44/42;* **6,7**

Cross the River Dee and go due S by the Fungle Road. The first part is a steep road to a cottage, The Guard, then a track continues through open woodland and across the Allt Dinnie to join a track which goes S over the col SW of Carnferg to Birse Castle. Leave this track before reaching the castle and turn S at a SRWS signpost to follow a well-marked path to another SRWS signpost at 521900.

At this point the walker can go N and E *via* Ballochan Farm and Birse Church to Forest of Birse. The main route continues SSW keeping on the W side of the stream up to the col between Mudlee Bracks and Tampie.

800 metres beyond the col the path is joined by the Fir Mounth (route 171) and descends by Shinfur and the Water of Tarf to Tarfside. The road to Edzell follows the left bank of the River North Esk, but for walkers a better route is to cross the North Esk at Tarfside and go down its right bank by Keenie and Dalhastnie to Gannochy Bridge. Then turn down the path on the river bank from the bridge to reach Edzell, 20 km from Tarfside.

Note: Balfour calls this route the Forest of Birse Mounth, 'from Cairn Corse to Birse on Deeside'. Cairncross is at Tarfside. The route is shown on Roy's map.

171 Dinnet to Tarfside (The Fir Mounth)
21km/13mls   Maps: OS 44/42; **6,7**

From Dinnet the route is across the River Dee and SE by Tillycairn and over Belrorie Hill to the old bridge over the Water of Tanar at Millfield, which can also be reached from Aboyne by Bridge o' Ess. On the road near Tillycairn a stone erected in the last century by Sir William Brooks of Glentanar describes this crossing incorrectly as the route used by Edward I in 1296. From the bridge over the Tanar go S until opposite Glentanar House, then climb gradually through the woods and up the Burn of Skinna.

In about 2½km cross the Burn of Skinna and climb the ridge between it and the Water of Allachy to Craigmahandle (574m). After a slight drop the path rises again to St. Colme's Well, and goes just W of the summit of Gannoch (731m) and S over Tampie (723m). 1½km further S the path joins the Fungle Road on its descent to Tarfside and Edzell.

Note: Balfour calls this route Mounth Gammel. There is a Gamel's Path across the Cheviots.

172 Ballater to Tarfside by Mount Keen
26km/16mls   *Maps: OS 44/42;* **6,7**

Cross the River Dee and go SW along the B976 for 1km to Bridge of Muick. Strike uphill to the left by a narrow road to Balintober, and continue by a track which climbs S then SE round the side of Craig Vallich to a col on its S side. Descend a short distance and go E to cross the headwaters of the Pollagach Burn and climb to a gate in the fence at 600m on the ridge opposite. Beyond it the track descends, first E then S to a footbridge over the Water of Tanar. This point can also be reached from Dinnet by road up Glen Tanar. The track climbs S up the N ridge of Mount Keen (939m) and reaches 750m on its W side. An alternative path goes over the summit.

Continue S and in 1½km the track begins to drop steeply by the Ladder Burn to the cottage of Glenmark, beyond which is the well commemorating Queen Victoria's crossing by this route in 1861. The track continues down the E bank of the Water of Mark to the road at Invermark, 6km W of Tarfside.

173 Ballater to Clova (The Capel Mounth)
31km/19mls   *Maps: OS 44/42;* **6,7**

Go by road up Glen Muick for 14km to the Spittal of Glenmuick, the site of an old hospice for travellers. 400 metres further a track strikes diagonally uphill S across the W side of Black Hill and then continues SSW over undulating moorland W of Watery Hill to Gallow Hillock. From there the path climbs slightly over the shoulder of Capel Mounth and then descends steeply in zigzags down the ridge between Moulzie Burn and Capel Burn and through a plantation to reach Glen Clova 1km N of Braedownie. From there Glen Doll youth hostel is ½km up the glen of that name, and Clova Inn is 5km down Glen Clova.

Note: This old route is marked as 'Mounth Capell' on a map dated about 1360.

174 Crathie to Clova
34km/21mls   *Maps: OS 44/42;* **6,7**

Although this is not strictly speaking a Mounth Path, it is included in this section as a variation of the Capel Mounth.

Starting at Crathie, go along the B976 road to Easter Balmoral and the distillery. Turn S at 272938 and go SE along a road to a deer fence and gate at 276933. Continue SE then S along a good track round the E slope of Tom Bad a' Mhonaidh to the col S of Meall Gorm. At the col take the right-hand track which leads directly to Allt-na-giubhsaich, and cross the glen to Spittal of Glenmuick.

At this point the Capel Mount route is joined and may be followed to Clova as described above. An alternative way goes SW along a track just above Loch Muick for 3km and then climbs by steep zigzags to the level plateau above. Continue along the track on the edge of this plateau to the little hut at the col between Broad Cairn and Sandy Hillock. From there take the path S to Bachnagairn (ruin) at the head of Glen Clova. Go down the glen by a track to Braedownie and Clova Inn.

175 Braemar to Glen Clova (The Tolmount)
29km/18mls   *Maps: OS 43,44/41; 6*

Go S from Braemar by the A93 road for just over 3km to Auchallater, then SE up Glen Callater by a good track to Loch Callater. Continue along the path on the NE side of the loch and up the Allt an Loch with a steep climb up the headwall of Glen Callater to reach the col at 880m between Tolmount and Knaps of Fafernie. The path turns SE across the featureless plateau, climbs slightly to 900m just below the top of Crow Craigies and continues along the undulating crest of a broad ridge towards Craig Lunkard. Before reaching that point descend steeply S into the head of Glen Doll, but do not go right down to the White Water. The path passes a small shelter and continues SE for almost 2km (at this point it is called Jock's Road) before it drops down to the floor of the glen and enters the forest. Glen Doll youth hostel is 3km further on, and ½km beyond it routes 173 and 174 are joined 5km from Clova Inn.

This is one of the most serious routes described in this book. It crosses a high, exposed and featureless plateau which in winter is frequently swept by storms. At that time of year the path over the plateau is likely to be covered by snow for several months and route-finding in bad weather is very difficult.

This right of way was the subject of an action in the Court of Session in 1886-87, and in the House of Lords in 1888, when it was proved that it had been for long the practice of drovers to take sheep from Braemar over the Tolmount to the market at Cullow, near Kirriemuir.

176 Braemar to Glen Isla (The Monega Pass)

35km/22mls   *Maps: OS 43,44/41,49;* **6**

This route begins on the A93 Cairnwell road, 12km S of Braemar, near a footbridge over the Cairnwell Burn at 149800. From there go SE up the steepening slope of Sron na Gaoithe, where there is virtually no path up the grassy hillside. Continue SE along a broad ridge to reach the watershed of the Mounth range 1km N of Glas Maol where the indistinct path becomes a vehicle track. Follow it S towards the summit of this hill for about ½km, then bear SSE above the very steep slopes at the head of the Caenlochan Glen and 50m below and about 300 metres E of the top of Glas Maol. The track bears SE along the edge of the cliffs above the Caenlochan Glen over the slight rise of Little Glas Maol, then S (bypassing the summit of Monega Hill) and down to Glen Isla 1km above Tulchan Lodge. From there it is 15km down the glen by road to Kirkton of Glenisla.

The remarks about the serious nature of the Tolmount route, particularly in winter, apply equally well to the Monega Pass.

177 Blair Atholl to Braemar by Glen Tilt

44km/28mls   *Maps: OS 43/41,48;* **7,8**

The right of way from Blair Atholl goes by the road on the E side of the River Tilt to Fenderbridge, and then N by a path through natural woodland on the hillside above the river. The path descends past Croftmore to the river at Gilberts Bridge, and the way continues up the road past Marble Lodge, across the river and 4km further to Forest Lodge. Continue along the road, which 5km beyond Forest Lodge bears uphill to the left on its way to Tarf bothy.

The route to Braemar continues unmistakeably up Glen Tilt by a path which in 2½km crosses the Tarf Water by the Bedford Memorial Bridge, erected in 1886 as a memorial to a young Englishman drowned while trying to ford the Tarf. The Falls of Tarf are partly seen from the bridge. The path continues NE up the narrow glen of the Allt Garbh Buidhe and reaches the watershed at about 490m.

Continuing N from there, the landscape is very different, for the deep, straight and narrow trench of Glen Tilt changes to the more expansive rounded hills and open glens that hold the Bynack and Geldie burns on their way to join the River Dee. Go N along the wide glen of the Allt an t-Seilich past the ruins of Bynack Lodge to reach the Geldie Burn, where there is (in 1994) no bridge. Beyond there a rough track leads alongside the Geldie Burn to White Bridge, where the River Dee is crossed, and onwards beside the Dee to Linn of Dee, where the public road is reached, 10km from Braemar.

178 Blair Atholl or Calvine to Kingussie by the Minigaig Pass
45km/28mls   *Maps: OS 35,42,43/37,48;* **5,8**
From Blair Atholl go up the E side of the River Tilt to the old bridge, cross it to Old Blair and then go NW by the road up the Banvie Burn. In another 2½km turn N up the Allt na Moine Baine for 1km, then cross this burn and go NW over to the Allt an t-Seapail and then, still NW, over to the Allt Sheicheachan, where the track ends at a bothy. Continue NNW along an indistinct path round the hillside, descend into Glen Bruar and go up to Bruar Lodge, where the track from Calvine is joined. (This track, which starts from the A9 road 7km W of Blair Atholl, can be used as an alternative start to the Minigaig Pass).

From Bruar Lodge, continue up the E bank of the Bruar Water for another 5km and when the glen divides strike up the steep hill straight ahead (due N) to reach the crest of Uchd a' Chlarsair. Descend slightly, still heading N, and climb a gradual slope to the Minigaig Pass (833m). The descent across the W slopes of Leathad an Taobhain continues N, then lower down the path bears NW down the N bank of the Allt Bhran to join the private road in Glen Tromie. (At this point route 179 is joined).

The route down Glen Tromie for the next 5km goes along the road, and then there are two possible finishes. The original route to Ruthven Barracks and Kingussie crosses the River Tromie and goes steeply uphill over the E shoulder of Sron na Gaoithe onto the high undulating moorland on the W side of the glen. It continues NNE, the path becoming more distinct until at 770974 it joins a well-defined path which leads NNW down the hillside to Ruthven Barracks, 1km from Kingussie.

The alternative finish goes right down Glen Tromie to Tromie Bridge, 4km along the B970 road from Kingussie. The direct route from Glentromie Lodge to Ruthven Barracks by the path over Beinn Bhuidhe is not a right of way.

The Minigaig is the only road to the north shown on Greene's map of 1689 and Moll's map of 1725. It was superseded by the military road over the Drumochter Pass constructed by Wade in 1728-30, although after that date the Minigaig still appeared on maps as a 'summer road to Ruthven'.

If doing this route from Ruthven Barracks southwards, the start is at a field gate about 50 metres SW of the carpark at the barracks. Go along the edge of a field, turn right along the edge of the next field and aim S along a track up a small wooded valley to a ruined cottage, beyond which a stile gives access across a fence to the open hillside. Higher up, on the crest of the moor, look out for the point where the right of way turns SSW while the more obvious path continues SE to Glentromie Lodge.

179 Dalnacardoch to Tromie Bridge by the Gaick Pass
31km/19mls   *Maps: OS 35,42/37,48;* **8**
Dalnacardoch is 11km NW of Calvine on the A9 road. A private road goes N through a plantation past a radio mast and continues N beside the Edendon Water for 8km to Sronphadruig Lodge. ½km beyond the lodge leave the track and follow a path N along the W side of Loch an Duin, across the foot of the very steep slopes of An Dun which plunge for 300m from its summit into the loch.

At the head of Loch an Duin go NE across the glen to reach the start of a track which continues down the E side of the Allt Loch an Duin, past Loch Bhrodainn, Gaick Lodge and Loch an t-Seilich to join route 178. The N end of the Gaick Pass route can finish either at Ruthven Barracks or Tromie Bridge, as described above for route 178.

SECTION 15

The Cairngorms and Northeast Scotland

180 Kingussie to Braemar by Glen Feshie
51km/32mls   *Maps: OS 35,43/37,41; **7,8***

From Kingussie cross the River Spey and go E by Ruthven Barracks to Tromie Bridge and Drumguish, where a track goes SE uphill across open moorland and through forest to the Allt Chomhraig. Cross this burn by a bridge to Baileguish and continue E by Corarnstilmore to Glen Feshie. Alternatively, from Kincraig or Kingussie go by road to Insh House and up the W side of Glen Feshie to the same point.

Continue up Glen Feshie by the private road to Carnachuin and cross to the E bank of the river by a footbridge. Follow the track (in places a path) along the NE bank of the River Feshie through fine old pine woods and below the steep crags and screes of Creag na Gaibhre. About 11km from Carnachuin, the River Eidart is reached. Go upstream for several hundred metres to cross this potentially dangerous river by a bridge at 914886 and a short distance beyond it resume an easterly course to cross the watershed to the N bank of the Geldie Burn. About 5km beyond the Eidart the road from Geldie Lodge (ruin) is joined, and the route is then down the Geldie, in a further 5km joining the path from Glen Tilt, route 177 . Continue NE to White Bridge and the River Dee, which is followed to the Linn of Dee, Inverey and Braemar.

181 Braemar to Aviemore by the Lairig Ghru
51km/28mls   *Maps: OS 36,43/37,41; **7,8***

This great pass is the most frequented route through the Cairngorms, passing through much grander scenery than the Glen Feshie or Lairig an Laoigh routes. It is a long strenuous walk, requiring 10 to 12 hours, on a well trodden path marked by cairns on its higher reaches. The walking distance can be shortened by starting from Inverey (8km W of Braemar), where accommodation can usually be obtained in one of the cottages, as well as in the youth hostel.

From Braemar go W by road through Inverey to the Linn of Dee, and then back along the N bank of the Dee for 800m to Glen Lui and NW up this glen to Derry Lodge. (Alternatively, before reaching Inverey cross to Mar Lodge and go left to Glen Lui). From Derry Lodge the path goes W along the N bank of the Luibeg Burn, crossing this burn where it comes down from Ben Macdui by a footbridge just upstream, and continues W over a broad col into Glen Dee opposite The Devil's Point. Corrour Bothy is seen across the Dee. The route is now N up Glen Dee, passing on the left Cairn Toul, the great cliffs of An Garbh Choire, and then Braeriach. On the right are the slopes of Ben Macdui. The path passes the Pools of Dee, one of the sources of the River Dee, and reaches the rough boulder strewn summit of the pass (833m).

The descent to Speyside is at first on the W side of the Allt Druidh, but below the site of the now demolished Sinclair Memorial Hut (959037) the path crosses to the E side of the stream and leads down to the first scattered pines of the Forest of Rothiemurchus.

If aiming for Glenmore, the best route is to follow the path branching to the right from a point just below the site of the demolished hut. It leads N on a gradual ascent to the Creag a' Chalamain gap and then goes NE to cross the Allt Mor by the bridge near the reindeer enclosure and joins the ski road 2½km SE of Loch Morlich.

As the first trees of Rothiemurchus Forest are reached, another branch path goes right to Rothiemurchus Lodge, from where a private road leads down to the W end of Loch Morlich. This is the shortest finish to reach a public road.

The traditional Lairig Ghru path goes down through the forest on the NE side of the Allt Druidh to an important junction of paths at 938076 where a right turn leads NE to the W end of Loch Morlich, and a left turn leads in 1km to the Cairngorm Club footbridge, erected in 1912, and in a further 3km to Coylumbridge, 2½km from Aviemore.

In the reverse direction, starting from Aviemore, there are signposts at Coylumbridge and 800 metres further on where the

Lairig Ghru and Gleann Einich paths diverge. At the crossing of paths at 938076 turn right. After passing the Pools of Dee, follow the left bank of the River Dee, and just after the Corrour Bothy footbridge take the left-hand path which goes slightly uphill and over a col to Glen Luibeg and Derry Lodge. This is slightly shorter and easier going than the route down the River Dee to White Bridge

W.J.Watson in *Place Names of Celtic Scotland* considers ghru to be a corruption of druidh, the stream flowing N from the pass.

182 Braemar to Nethy Bridge by the Lairig an Laoigh

48km/30mls   *Maps: OS 36,43/38; 7*

As far as Derry Lodge the way is the same as route 181 for the Lairig Ghru. Just beyond the lodge cross the footbridge and continue up Glen Derry, at first on the W side of the Derry Burn, then on the E side. At the foot of Coire Etchachan the path to Ben Macdui strikes off to the left. For Nethybridge keep straight on up to the pass (745m) and descend by the Dubh Lochan to the Fords of Avon, where the ford may be quite deep and dangerous in spate conditions.

Keeping N, the path in another 2km passes Lochan a' Bhainne and reaches the headwaters of the Water of Caiplich, which flows down to Tomintoul. Care must be taken to follow the path when it goes uphill over the E shoulder of Bynack More at a height of 774m. From there the route is NW across the wide slopes of Coire Odhar and over the highest point of the route at 790m on the N ridge of Bynack More, then a descent of 350m leads to the River Nethy. Cross the Nethy by the footbridge at Bynack Stable and follow a track WNW past Loch a Gharbh-Choire. Just beyond there the track forks; the left-hand branch leads SW through Ryvoan Pass by the picturesque An Lochan Uaine to Glenmore Lodge, Loch Morlich and Aviemore; the other track to the right goes N by Ryvoan Bothy to Forest Lodge, where roads and tracks are numerous, but by keeping N there is no difficulty in reaching Nethy Bridge.

In the reverse direction there is little to choose between Nethy Bridge and Aviemore as a starting point. The route from Aviemore by Loch Morlich through the Ryvoan Pass is only about 1½km longer than that from Nethy Bridge to the junction of tracks S of Ryvoan Bothy where the two routes meet. If the bus service from Aviemore to Loch Morlich is used, this route is much shorter.

The N end of this route gives a good shorter walk from Loch Morlich to Nethy Bridge (15km). Go past Glenmore Lodge and An Lochan Uaine, keep left to Ryvoan Bothy and continue through the fine old pines of Abernethy Forest to Forest Lodge and Nethy Bridge.

183 Coylumbridge to Achlean (Glen Feshie) by Gleann Einich
20km/12¹/₂mls   *Maps: OS 36/37;* **8**

   This route crosses the hills between Loch Einich and Glen Feshie, and it involves the ascent (or descent) of a steep little corrie. It is only suitable for those with mountaineering experience, particularly in winter and spring when the hills are snow-covered. In summer, however, it should present no problems.

   From Coylumbridge go S along the Lairig Ghru path, but keep right in 800 metres to pass below Whitewell (where this route may be started) and continue along the track up Gleann Einich. The crossing of the Beanaidh Beag may be difficult in spate, particularly in spring when snow in the high corries of Braeriach is melting. At the outflow of Loch Einich go round the W side of the loch along a path which follows the lochside below the crags of Sgor Gaoith.

   The path makes a rising traverse above the S end of Loch Einich and peters out at a little stream flowing down from the plateau at Fuaran Diotach. Climb up steeply beside this stream to reach the plateau 1km NE of Carn Ban Mor (1052m). Cross this very flat-topped hill and continue SW from the summit for 400 metres to join a path leading NW down towards Glen Feshie. The path goes along the spur towards Carn Ban Beag and then down the slopes on the N side of the Allt Fhearnagan to Achlean at the end of the public road on the E side of Glen Feshie.

184 Nethy Bridge to Tomintoul
20km/12¹/₂mls   *Maps: OS 36/38;* **7**

   (a) Go from Nethy Bridge along the Tomintoul road for 5km and then take the right-hand fork which goes to Dorback Lodge. Go to the left behind the lodge past Fae to Letteraitten and then continue E by an old road to the Burn of Brown, which must be crossed at a shallow ford. From there a path leads down the E side of the burn to meet a forestry road which goes E uphill and past Stronachavie to join the A939 road at Bridge of Avon, 2¹/₂km NW of Tomintoul.

An alternative is to take the left-hand fork just beyond Fae and continue NE by a good track above the Allt Iomadaidh gorge to Bridge of Brown, 6½km NW of Tomintoul.

(b) For a longer (8km) and more difficult route to Dorback Lodge, take the road on the SW bank of the River Nethy to Forest Lodge. Just before reaching the Lodge cross to the E bank of the river and go by a forest road, first SE for 800m, then S for nearly 2km. There turn E round the southern slope of Carn a' Chnuic, passing on the N of Loch a' Chnuic and then head E for a narrow pass, the Eag Mhor. From there go down the slope to the Dorback Burn and Dorback Lodge, and continue as in (a) to Tomintoul.

185 Braemar to Tomintoul
32km/20mls   *Maps: OS 36,43/38; 7*

(a) Go E from Braemar along the A93 road for 5km to Invercauld Bridge and shortly beyond it take the side road left to Keiloch. Continue straight on by that road NW towards the back of Invercauld House. After approximately 1½km (ie before reaching Invercauld House) take the steep track on the right uphill heading N by the W side of Meall Gorm and the E of Creag a' Chait to the Bealach Dearg (shelter) at 180981. There either take the foopath N down the Allt na Claise Moire to the River Gairn or continue along the track to the Gairn. Cross the footbridge and go along the N side of the Gairn, then N by the E side of Loch Builg and down Glen Builg to Inchrory, 11km from Tomintoul.

(b) Go to Keiloch as in (a), but there turn right (instead of left), and go NE to Felagie, and N for another 2½km by Balnoe to Balmore. (This may be shortened by starting from Inver on the A93 and going *via* Knockan to Balnoe).

Turn E at Balmore across the Fearder Burn and follow the path to Ratlich. Keep on an old track E then N, keeping to the E of Carn Moine an Tighearn, then NW along the E slope of Culardoch, and descend in another 5km by Tom a' Chuir to the River Gairn and Loch Builg to join (a) above.

(c) A much longer way is to take the Lairig an Laoigh (route 182) to the Fords of Avon, and then go down the river by its N bank (path at first, then track) past Faindouran Bothy to Inchrory to join (a).

186 Crathie to Tomintoul

35km/22mls   *Maps: OS 36,37/38; **7***

For most of its length this is an old drove road between Deeside and Tomintoul. From Crathie to Glen Gairn it is also the Old Military Road constructed in 1750-54.

From Crathie follow the A93 road towards Braemar for 400 metres, then go N by the B976 for about 1½km until just beyond Bush Crathie. There take a track going off to the left and go N by the W of Blairglass and then NW down to the River Gairn. Descend the Gairn for 2km and then cross it to Easter Sleach. (This point may also be reached by a shorter walk from Braenaloin on the B976 road). From Easter Sleach go due N over Tom Odhar and Carn Mor (the drove road is here called the Camus Road) to Ordgarff and Cock Bridge. Then go W up the N bank of the River Don for 3½km to Dunanfiew, and from there N over the hill between Carn Ealasaid and Tolm Buirich, and down to Blairnamarrow on the Lecht road, 6km SE of Tomintoul.

An alternative after passing Blairglass is to go up the River Gairn to Loch Builg and continue by route 185 to Inchrory and Tomintoul.

187 Ballater to Cock Bridge

19km/12mls   *Maps: OS 37/39; **7***

(a) Leave Ballater by the road to Braemar and at Bridge of Gairn turn to the right up the road on the E bank of the Gairn to Lary. Continue by path up Glen Fenzie to the Glas Choille road, the Old Military Road which crosses to Donside. 1½km beyond the summit of this road, strike left by a path across the Burn of Tornahaish to a bend in the River Don, and up its S bank to Cock Bridge.

(b) For an alternative go up the left bank of the River Gairn from Lary to the bridge on the A939 road, and continue for another 2km to Tullochmacarrick. 'The Ca' Road' runs N from there to the Allt Coire nam Freumh; its continuation N is now lost where it climbs over the ridge between Carn a' Bhacain (751m) and The Ca' (678m) to join (a) 400 metres SE of Delavine at 205068.

Note: Routes 186 and 187 are shown as an old road from Corgarff to Crathie on a rough map in the British Museum drawn by George Campbell, Cadet Gunner, about 1748.

188 Cock Bridge (Donside) to Tomintoul by Inchrory
22¹/₂km/14mls   *Maps: OS 36,37/38; 7*
By rough road up the S side of the River Don to Inchrory, and then N by the estate road down Glen Avon to Tomintoul.

189 Cock Bridge (Donside) to Nethy Bridge
51¹/₂km/32mls   *Maps: OS 36,37/38; 7*
Follow route 188 to Inchrory, then go W by track, later a path, up the River Avon past Faindouran Bothy. Reach the Lairig an Laoigh (route 182) at Fords of Avon and turn N to follow this route to Nethy Bridge.

190 Ballater to Strathdon
22¹/₂km/14mls   *Maps: OS 37/39; 7*
Follow route 187 up the River Gairn to Lary, then go NE up the road to Morven Lodge. Leave it in 2¹/₂km (at 342023) to go right for 500 metres by a track to 344027 and thence up the Morven Burn to the col on the NW side of Morven (872m). Then go down the E side of the Deskry Water to Boultenstone (Inn) and the Strathdon road.

From a point about 3km N of Lary (at 344027) a track goes E across the S slopes of Morven, mostly at about the 500m contour, and drops down the E side of Morven to Milton of Whitehouse, from where Dinnet or Tarland can be reached by minor roads.

191 Tarland to Glenkindie (Donside)
14¹/₂km/9mls   *Maps: OS 37/39; 7*
(a) From Tarland go NW by road for 3¹/₂km to East Davoch, then E to Bog Farm. There strike up the hillside, at first NE, then due N by Humphrey's Well and along the W slope of the Socach (an old drove road) to the top of Craiglea Hill. Then descend the NW ridge to Chapel of Towie, and thence W by road to Glenkindie in Strathdon.

(b) For an alternative route from East Davoch, which gives fine views over the Howe of Cromar and towards Morven, take the cart track NW towards Lazy Well and continue past the E side of Baderonach Hill to the road from Towie to Rippachie. From there take the minor public road to Glenkindie.

192 Alford to Rhynie
18km/11mls   *Maps: OS 37/39; 7*

From Alford go N by the public road to Montgarrie and Tullynessle, then NW by Dubston and the old quarry road to Correen Quarry, now abandoned. From there continue over the Correen Hills between Badingair Hill and Mire of Midgates to Cairn More and the road to Rhynie.

193 Strathdon to Cabrach
18km/11mls   *Maps: OS 37/39; 7*

From Glenkindie in Strathdon go N up the Kindie Burn by Glencuie and Rinmore to Largue, where the road ends. Then go NW by track and path over the W slope of Glenlaff Hill to join another road about 1½km N of the summit. This road leads down the Kindie Burn to Powneed Farm, from where a farm road goes to Cabrach.

194 Strathdon to Dufftown
35½km/22mls   *Maps: OS 28,37/39,29; 7*

From a point 2km E of Strathdon (370123) go N by road *via* Kirkton of Glenbuchat and NW up the Water of Buchat to Upperton. Continue N by the track on the E side of White Hill to pass the summit (466m) at 361201 and onwards by Roch Ford and the E side of Keirn Hill, where several other recent tracks cross the old one, to reach Aldivalloch, 2km W of Cabrach village.

From Aldivalloch go W over Dead Wife's Hillock; there is a track to the deer fence near the top of the hill. Continue W to the Black Water and follow the track N down the E bank and ford the river to Blackwater Lodge. Continue N by the private road on the E slope of Scaut Hill for 4km, and by path N on the E of Carn Chrom to the road bridge over the River Fiddich at Bridgehaugh, thence N to Dufftown.

195 Strathdon to Tomintoul by The Ladder Road
26m/16mls   *Maps: OS 36,37/38,39; 7*

Start from Bellabeg ½km from Strathdon and go along the road up the NE side of the Water of Nochty to Auchernach and W through the forest to Aldachuie. 1km further the edge of the forest is reached and the burn crossed to Duffdefiance. The route continues NW uphill by a path, joining a track over Finlate Hill, and finally by a path to the summit of the Ladder Road (735m) at the col just NE of Dun Muir. Descending on the NW side, a good path leads down into the wide bowl of the Braes of Glenlivet at Ladderfoot. From there go by road to Corry and Chapeltown and on past Clashnoir to Lettoch. Continue SW by path over the hill and through the forestry plantation to Inchnacape and the B9008 road about 4km from Tomintoul.

196 Tomintoul to Cabrach by The Steplar
27km/17mls   *Maps: OS 36,37/38,39; 7*
This is an old right of way and drove road. From Tomintoul take the B9008 Dufftown road and at 4km (about 130 metres past the road leading to Inchnacape farm) a gate on the right opens onto the track which goes over the hill, through the Forestry plantation, to Lettoch. (To this point the route is the reverse of 195). From Lettoch go to Burnside of Thain, from where a track goes NE over to the River Livet and joins another track to Suie, now deserted. About 200 metres beyond Suie bear right, leaving the better road which carries on up Glen Suie, and follow a rough old cart road, meeting in about 3km a new road which has been bulldozed and leads E to the ford at the Black Water. From there to the deer fence near the top of the Dead Wife's Hillock the path is in places difficult to find, but there is a tractor road E from the deer fence leading down to Aldivalloch (supposed scene of the song *Roy's Wife of Aldivalloch*), and from there to Cabrach there is a good road.

Routes 195 and 196 are described in more detail in the Scottish Mountaineering Club guidebook *The Cairngorms* by Adam Watson.

197 Tomintoul to Dufftown by Glen Fiddich
37km/23mls   *Maps: OS 28,36,37/29,38; 7*
Follow route 196 to Suie, and continue NE up Glen Suie by a track which at the head of the glen goes off up Corryhabbie Hill. Continue by a path over the watershed and down the River Fiddich to the bridge near Glenfiddich Lodge, and on to Bridgehaugh, thence by the road or by Smithstown to Dufftown.

198 Tomintoul to Ballindalloch and Elgin

53km/33mls   *Maps: OS 28,36/29,38; 7*

Take the B9008 road from Tomintoul for 1km, then go N by the minor road past Croughly for 3km. Turn right past Glenconglass and Ellick and go down the Chabet Water to Ballenlish and the bridge over the River Avon. Cross to the W bank and go down the river; there is a track as far as Lyne, but therafter the way is more difficult to follow as far as Dalrachie where good tracks lead to Bridge of Avon, 21km/13mls from Tomintoul.

To continue to Elgin go N by road to Knockando, then NNE past Mannoch Cottage and along the W side of Elchies Forest. Continue N over the moors on the E side of Carn na Cailliche and the W side of Pikey Hill past Lochbuie to reach Shougle. Finally, go from there to Elgin along a minor road.

199 Grantown-on-Spey to Tomintoul by Cromdale

22½km/14mls   *Maps: OS 36/38; 7*

Take the B9102 road for 2km NE from Grantown-on-Spey to the crossroads at 055293, then turn right on a minor road to cross the River Spey and reach Cromdale. Continue SE by a track up the Haughs of Cromdale round a plantation (Claggersnich Wood), then climb steeply SE to cross the Hills of Cromdale about 2km N of Creagan a' Chaise. Descend SE to Milton and continue S by a minor road on the W side of the River Avon to reach the A939 near Bridge of Avon, 3km from Tomintoul.

SECTION 16
Moray and the Monadhliath

200 Grantown-on-Spey to Forres
35km/22mls   *Maps: OS 27,36/ 29; 7*

This is a long walk following moorland tracks and minor roads across the eastern part of Dava Moor and down into fine wooded country on the E of the Findhorn River. The first 3½km of the walk is along the A939 road N from Grantown to Cottartown. Then go along the minor road past Lynmore and Lagg until within ½km of Auchnagallin, and turn N along a track leading up onto Dava Moor past Huntly's Cave. The track leads past the ruin of Badahad to the headwaters of the Ourack Burn, and then there are 2km of pathless moorland down the burn to join another track. Continue N on this track down the River Divie and past Shenvault, Lurg and Johnstripe on the E side of Hill of Glaschyle to reach Tomnamoon. Proceed thence by minor roads past Craigroy, through Altyre Woods, and past Wardend House and the distillery at Manachie to reach Forres.

Most parts of the old railway from Grantown-on-Spey to Forres are still walkable. The line is just W of the walk described above

201 Dulnain Bridge or Grantown-on-Spey to Dava by Lochindorb
18km/11mls   *Maps: OS 27,36/ 29,38; 7,8*

This walk, much shorter that the preceding one, crosses the SW corner of Dava Moor from the Spey valley to Lochindorb. One very convenient starting point is 2km W of Dulnain Bridge on the A938 road. Go N along the minor road past Achnahannet and continue up the track which ends at the ruined cottage of Easter Rynechkra. A path leads N for a short distance further, but it soon disappears in the rough moorland. Once past the scattered pines N of Easter Rynechkra bear NW across a flat col and descend NNW down the E side of Loch an t-Sidhein to its outflow. A short distance further NW the start of a grassy track is reached and this leads down to the S end of Lochindorb. Finally, go NE along the minor road on the SE side of the loch to reach Dava on the A939 road.

An alternative start can be made from Grantown-on-Spey. From the centre of the town go NW up a minor road to Dreggie, and continue by the track which climbs NW across the SW side of Gorton Hill. From the end of the track climb WNW to reach the col N of Easter Rynechkra and continue as described above.

202 Dulsie to Tomatin by the River Findhorn
21km/13mls   *Maps: OS 27,35/28;* **8**
From the road junction just N of Dulsie (at 933418), take the minor road up the Findhorn valley to Drynachan Lodge and Daless. From there a track crosses a ford (at 860381) to the south bank of the River Findhorn and continues upstream to Ballachronin and then on by the path to Shenachie. Recross the Findhorn by ropeway and go by a track on the N bank to Ruthven, then on by minor road to join the A9 road 2km N of the Freeburn Hotel, Tomatin.

203 Boat of Garten to Tomatin by the Wade road
18km/11mls   *Maps: OS 35,36/37;* **8**
From the Kinveachy road junction (at 913188) 3km W of Boat of Garten take the private road under the railway and immediately after crossing the A9 road (beware of high-speed traffic) turn right to follow the Wade road going NW uphill through the forest and continue for 5$\frac{1}{2}$km to cross the River Dulnain by the Sluggan Bridge. Turn W to Insharn and then N to the Slochd. There the realigned A9 is crossed to its N side and the old road is followed NW to the bridge over the River Findhorn at Raibeg, 1km from Tomatin.
Note: The Wade road was constructed in 1728-29.

204 Tomatin to Whitebridge
50km/31mls   *Maps: OS 34,35/28,37;* **8**
Go up the valley of the Findhorn by road to Colgnafearn Lodge and Dalbeg, and then WSW at first by a track and later by a path up the River Eskin to the narrow pass (650m) leading through to the head of Glen Markie, where the path ends at a bothy. Continue downstream on the north side of the Glenmarkie Burn to another bothy at 563080 where a path is joined which leads to Sronlairig Lodge. From there a road goes NW by Loch Killin to Whitebridge.

205 Carrbridge to Aviemore by the River Dulnain
26km/16mls   *Maps: OS 35/28,37;* **8**

Take the Dalnahaitnach road out of Carrbridge for 3km. Then at
875215 turn N and take the Old Wade Military Road (now a track)
to cross the River Dulnain at Sluggan Bridge and continue 3km W
to Insharn. There turn S and go by track to the monument on the
NW side of the Dulnain (opposite Dalnahaitnach). Follow the NW
bank of the river upstream for 5km by a track to the bridge at
813165, and cross it to go SE on the estate road over the E shoulder
of Geal-charn Mor and down to Lynwilg. Cross the new A9 road
and take the older road for the last 2km to Aviemore.

*Note: The bridge at Dalnahaitnach has been down for several
years and the bridge to Inverlaidnan is private.*

206 Kingussie to Tomatin by the River Findhorn
43½km/27mls   *Maps: OS 35/28,37;* **8**

From the centre of Kingussie take the road up the E side of the
Allt Mor through the golf course, cross the burn at Pitmain Lodge
and continue by the track to the col between Carn a' Bhothain
Mholaich and Carn an Fhreiceadain at 718070. Take care not to
descend by the stream flowing N from the col, but go WNW across
the N slopes of Carn a' Bhothain Mholaich (no path and difficult in
mist) to the next burn (at 694082), the Allt Glas a' Charbaid. Go NW
down it and by path down the Elrick Burn to Coignafearn Lodge,
from where a road goes down the River Findhorn to Tomatin. This
route is marked as a road in Roy's Map of 1755.

207 Kingussie to Laggan
22km/14mls   *Maps: OS 35/37;* **8**

Cross the Spey by the B970 road to Ruthven, then strike SW past
Knappach, Milehouse of Nuide, Lochan Odhar and Phones to
Etteridge along the line of Wade's Military Road. Cross the A9 road
and the railway at 682922, then go N across the River Truim to
Crubenbeg Farm. Turn W through a gate to a track which goes
round some old buildings, and a short distance further go N to the
public road at 678943 near Mains of Glentruim. Continue W along
this quiet road to Catlodge on the A889 road 2½km from Laggan.

208 Newtonmore to Laggan by Glen Banchor
16km/10mls   *Maps: OS 35/37;* **8**
From the SW end of Newtonmore take the public road up Glen Banchor for just over 2km to its end at the Allt a' Chaorainn. Continue across the burn and along a track to Glenballoch and then by footpath on the N bank of the River Calder to a bridge and bothy at 648984 (no path for last 400 metres). Turn S by the track through Srath an Eilich for 5km to Cluny Castle on the A86 road, 3km W of Laggan.

209 Laggan to Whitebridge
35km/22mls   *Maps: OS 34,35/36,37;* **8**
From Laggan follow the road on the N side of the River Spey W for 4km to the Spey Dam, then go N by track up Glen Markie for almost 5km until past the Piper's Burn. Cross the Markie Burn and climb NW up the hillside to the E of Lochan a' Choire (no path), and continue NW over the broad ridge to the N end of Loch na Lairige. Go NNW down the E bank of the Crom Allt, where a path is soon reached leading to Sronlairig Lodge, there joining route 204 for the last 11km to Whitebridge.

210 Laggan to Fort Augustus by the Corrieyairack Pass
40km/25mls   *Maps: OS 34,35/36,37;* **8,9**
The Corrieyairack road was made by General Wade in 1731 as a continuation of the road from Crieff to Dalnacardoch which continued across the Drumochter Pass to Dalwhinnie, where it divided, one branch going by Aviemore to Inverness (see route 203) and the other by Laggan to Fort Augustus. There was an old 'road' here before Wade's time; it is shown on a map of 1725 in the British Museum. It was by the Corrieyairack that Prince Charles Edward Stewart marched south after raising his standard at Glenfinnan. J. B. Salmond, in his *Wade in Scotland* (1938), quotes the Hon. Mrs Murray's description of her crossing by coach in 1798.
The old Wade road leaves the A86 2km SW of Laggan. After 2km it coincides with the present-day public road, which comes from Laggan along the N side of the Spey. (Another good starting point is at Kinloch Laggan, from where a track goes N to join the Wade

road). 10km from Laggan the road, now tarred almost to Melgarve, passes the old barracks and former inn at Garvamore and crosses the Spey by Garva Bridge (a Wade bridge) to the N bank, and continues to Melgarve. (About 90 metres up the burn just E of Melgarve there is another Wade bridge). The Corrieyairack track now leaves the Spey and begins the climb to the pass by the Allt Yairack, the last 330 metres in twelve zigzags. The 775m summit provides magnificent views, and there is a steep descent on the W side to the Allt Lagan a' Bhainne bridge, then down Glen Tarff high on the W side of the glen above the deep tree-lined gorge of the River Tarff, to Cullachy. On reaching the public road go right, then first left, to Fort Augustus.

211 Laggan to Spean Bridge by Glen Roy and Glen Gloy
53km/33mls   *Maps: OS 34,35/36,37; **8,9***

Follow the Corrieyairack, route 210, up the Spey for 18½km to Melgarve. (It is about 4km shorter starting from Kinloch Laggan). At Melgarve the route to Spean Bridge crosses the Allt Yairack (bridge down) and keeps W along the N bank of the Spey, passing Loch Spey, and crosses the low pass (350m) into Glen Roy. Go down the N bank of the River Roy for 7km to Leckroy, where there are good views of the famous Parallel Roads. Then, instead of turning SW down Glen Roy (route 212), go almost due W, cross the River Turret, and keep W up the Allt a' Chomhlain to the col (357m) which leads into Glen Gloy (where new plantation may obscure the track to Auchivarie). Descend this glen to the Old Wade Road and bridge beside Glenfintaig Lodge, from where it is 6½km S by the main road (bus) to Spean Bridge.

This is one of the old highways of the Highlands, once the main route between Speyside and Lochaber. It is shown on Moll's map of 1725 as going from Ruthven (Kingussie) to Mucomir at the south end of Loch Lochy, from where a road ran S to Fort William and N to Kilcumein (Fort Augustus). The Wade Road from Fort William to Fort Augustus was made in 1726.

Note: Both routes 210 and 211 are shown as roads on Roy's map of 1755.

212 Laggan to Roybridge by Glen Roy
48km/30mls   *Maps: OS 34,35/36,37;* **8,9**
     From Laggan Bridge or Kinloch Laggan follow route 211 to Glen
Roy and along the NW bank of the River Roy past Leckroy to Turret
Bridge. Continue along the road on the NW side of the river, passing
below the Parallel Roads, to Roybridge Station. Below Achavady in
Glen Roy there is a viewpoint with information about the Parallel
Roads, which are the levels of a series of ice-dammed lakes that
existed during the last Ice Age.

SECTION 17
Rannoch to Lochaber

213 Kinloch Rannoch to Dalnaspidal
19km/12mls   *Maps: OS 42/48; 5*

A drove road starts at Annat, on the N side of Loch Rannoch 2½km W of Kinloch Rannoch, and goes N up the E side of the Annat Burn for about 1km, then strikes first W and then NW for about 2km to the Allt a' Chreagain Odhair. There the road coming up from Craiganour Lodge on Loch Rannoch is joined and the direction is then due N to Duinish, then across the Allt Shallainn which may be difficult in spate. (The bridge at 614675 had been swept away in 1993). Continue N to Loch Garry, and finally along its W side by a track for 5km to Dalnaspidal. As the name Dalnaspidal implies, there was at one time a hospice or inn there.

Roy's map of 1755 shows two routes, one leaving Loch Rannoch near Annat and the other from Aulich (near Craiganour Lodge) and uniting at the south end of Loch Garry.

214 Loch Rannoch to Dalwhinnie by Loch Ericht
35km/22mls   *Maps: OS 42/37,47; 5,8*

From a point on the B846 road 300 metres N of Rannoch Lodge at the W end of Loch Rannoch a track goes NW through a small wood, and a path continues along the E side of another area of forest. The track resumes N along the W slopes of Meall Liath na Doire Mhoir and goes down to the SW end of Loch Ericht and the bridge over the Cam Chriochan. From there go N along the W side of the loch (path for about 2½km) to the Alder Burn and Benalder Cottage, which is an open bothy and may be a useful stopping point on this long walk. Continue along the lochside by a narrow and for much of the way virtually non-existent path which clings to the steep lower slopes of Beinn Bheoil along the water's edge to reach Ben Alder Lodge. From there a good track goes for the final 9km to Dalwhinnie.

Note: The route is marked on Roy's map of 1755.

Ben Nevis and Aonach Beag from Luibeilt (route 219)

The north-west end of the Corrieyairack Pass above Fort Augustus (route 210)

The right of way through Glen Affric to Kintail (route 256)

215 Loch Rannoch to Loch Laggan
40km/25mls   *Maps: OS 42/36,37,47;* **5,8**
   Follow route 214 to the Alder Burn, cross the burn and climb to the stalkers' path which goes NW above it to the Bealach Cumhann. (Prince Charlie's Cave is E of this path and above Benalder Cottage). Beyond the bealach (660m) the path turns NE to the Bealach Dubh (725m) between Ben Alder and Aonach Beag, and descends by the Allt a' Chaoil-reidhe to Loch Pattack. From the E side of the loch an estate road goes down the River Pattack (keep right when the road forks in 7km) to Gallovie and the Laggan road, 2km E of Kinloch Laggan.
   An alternative route is to climb N from Benalder Cottage past the site of Prince Charlie's Cave to the Bealach Breabag and descend by the path along the E side of Loch a' Bhealaich Bheithe down to the Allt a' Chaoil-reidhe 1km above Culra Lodge. At that point the preceding route is rejoined. This variation involves a little more climbing, but saves a few kilometres of distance.

216 Corrour Station to Dalwhinnie
37km/23mls   *Maps: OS 41,42/36,37;* **5,8**
   From the railway station proceed E along the private road on the SE shore of Loch Ossian to Corrour Shooting Lodge. Continue by the path to cross the footbridge over the Uisge Labhair, and go upstream for 6km to join route 215 before crossing the Bealach Dubh. Descend the Allt a' Chaoil-reidhe past Culra bothy and Loch Pattack to reach Ben Alder Lodge in 10km and continue by route 214 to Dalwhinnie. This long walk not only goes through splendid mountainous country, but also has the advantage that it goes from one railway station to another.

217 Rannoch Station to Loch Ossian and Corrour Station
18km/11mls   *Maps: OS 41,42/ 47;* **5**
   Go E along the B846 road for 2½km to Loch Eigheach, and at 446578 take the track which goes NW. This track is part of The Road to the Isles, and leads in 3km to a crossing of the Allt Eigheach. Beyond there follow the path NW across the lower slopes of Carn Dearg and past the stark ruins of Corrour Old Lodge, which after it ceased to be used as a shooting lodge was for a few years used as an isolation hospital. No more isolated place can be imagined.

Follow the path as it swings N towards Loch Ossian, and before reaching the plantation above the loch turn W to descend to the head of Loch Ossian where the youth hostel of the same name stands on a promontory by the lochside. Corrour Station is a further 1½km along a road, and from there one can return to the day's starting point by train, provided one has consulted the timetable beforehand.

218 Corrour Station (Loch Ossian) to Tulloch Station
25km/15½mls   *Maps: OS 41,42/ 36,47; 9*
Follow the road along the SE shore of Loch Ossian to Corrour Shooting Lodge. Continue N along the road down Srath Ossian to Strathossian House, and then follow the path which climbs N round the shoulder of Meall Dhearcaig and continues W along the upper edge of the forest, gradually dropping to Fersit. From there go 3½km along the narrow public road to join the main A86 in Glen Spean 1½km W of Tulloch Station.

219 Corrour Station (Loch Ossian) to Glen Nevis and Fort William
29km/18mls or 33km/20½mls   *Maps: OS 41/47; 9*
This is a very fine walk through the heart of the highest mountains of Lochaber. It can be done from one youth hostel to another, Loch Ossian to Glen Nevis, or from one station to another, Corrour to Fort William.
From Corrour follow the path and then the track beside the West Highland Railway down to the head of Loch Treig and round to Creaguaineach Lodge. From there go up the Abhainn Rath by the path on its N side as far as Luibeilt where the crossing of the stream may be difficult in wet weather. Continue for a further 2½km to the watershed at Tom an Eite. The going is often very wet and boggy.
Once past Tom an Eite the path goes down the N side of the Water of Nevis past the ruins of Steall cottage to reach the gorge where the river rushes through a narrow rocky ravine. The path clings to the right-hand bank of the river along narrow ledges and through trees to reach the end of the public road in Glen Nevis where there is a carpark. The walk continues down the road in the glen past Polldubh to reach the youth hostel, 29km from Corrour

Station. A further 4km along the Glen Nevis road leads to Fort William.

220 Corrour Station (Loch Ossian) to Spean Bridge
25km/15½mls   *Maps: OS 41/36,47;* **9**
   Follow route 219 for its first 6km as far as Creaguaineach Lodge. From there go NW then N by the path on the W side of the Allt na Lairige through the Lairig Leacach. At the Lairig Leacach bothy a track is reached and it leads over the watershed and down the Allt Leachdach, through a short section of forest and down to Corriechoille. From there follow the minor road on the S side of the River Spean for 4km to Spean Bridge. Like the preceding route, this one goes from one station to another on the West Highland Line.
   This route is part of the old drove road from the Great Glen to Rannoch and the south. Lairig Leacach means 'pass of the flagstones'.

221 Kinlochleven to Corrour Station (Loch Ossian)
24km/15mls   *Maps: OS 41/47;* **9**
   Go E from Kinlochleven up the N bank of the River Leven to the Blackwater Reservoir, and 1 km E of the dam strike NE up the Allt an Inbhir. Continue beyond this burn NE to Loch Chiarain, up the Allt Feith Chiarain and down Gleann Iolairean to the head of Loch Treig. This is the line of an old drove road that was used before the creation of the Blackwater Reservoir. From the head of Loch Treig go SE by the track and path alongside the West Highland Railway to reach Corrour Station.

222 Kinlochleven to Spean Bridge
30km/18½mls   *Maps: OS 41/36,47;* **9**
   From the N end of Kinlochleven take the path which crosses a burn and climbs steeply NE to join the track leading to Loch Eilde Mor. Go NE along this track past lochs Eilde Mor and Eilde Beag to Luibeilt where route 219 is crossed. Cross the Abhainn Rath, which may be difficult if the river is in spate, and continue N by the path up the Allt nam Fang. Cross the pass between Meall Mor and Stob Ban and descend to the Lairig Leacach bothy, where route 220 is

joined and followed over the Lairig Leacach, down to Corriechoille and along the road to Spean Bridge.

An alternative and slightly shorter (in distance) finish to this route can be made from the Lairig Leacach bothy by climbing NE for a short distance to cross a col and descend by Coire na Cabaig to Coire Laire. This glen is long and pathless, but the going on the NW side of the Allt Laire is not too difficult and leads to a forest road which in turn leads past Inverlair to the A86 road 1½km W of Tulloch Station.

223 Kinlochleven to Fort William
20km/12½mls   *Maps: OS 41/46,47;* **9**

Leave Kinlochleven by the B863 road on the N side of Loch Leven as far as the school. From there follow the path which climbs NW up the wooded hillside , cross the private road to Mamore Lodge and higher up join the track from the lodge that leads W up the Allt Nathrach. The track leads over a pass at about 330m, and descends to Lairigmor. The way to Fort William continues along this track which swings N and in a further 4km becomes a narrow public road leading down to Fort William.

This route is part of the West Highland Way, and is also on the line of the Old Military Road that was constructed by General Caulfield in 1749-50 from Fort William southwards over the Devil's Staircase.

From Lairigmor a path, which is a right of way, leads SW over the W ridge of Mam na Gualainn and descends to the B863 road on the N side of Loch Leven at Callert House.

Another finish to this walk is possible from Blar a' Chaorainn where the public road is joined at 100666. From there go W to Lundavra and then SW past the head of Lochan Lunn Da Bhra. Continue SW across a flat col (no path for 1½km) to the edge of the Glenrigh Forest where a road is joined. Follow this road on the true right-hand bank of the Abhainn Righ for 5km until a bridge on the left leads across the river and down to Onich.

SECTION 18
Ardgour, Sunart and Moidart

224 Drimnin to Strontian
43km/27mls   *Maps: OS 40,47,49/ 45,46;* **10**

From Drimnin on the Sound of Mull near the end of the B849 road from Lochaline, go uphill by a narrow road to Mungosdail. Just beyond there take a track into the forest and follow it uphill for 1½km. Just after crossing a burn look for a smaller path going NE for about 1½km to the edge of the forest at a gate. Continue NE over a ridge (no path) above and to the E of Lochan Chrois Bheinn and descend to enter another forest at 601550. Go down a path through the forest on the W side of the Barr River to join a track which leads SE for 3½km to the head of Loch Teacuis. Go round the head of the loch by road until about 1½km NW of Kinloch, and at that point follow a path E then N across the Bealach Sloc an Eich and down through forest to Glencripesdale.

From that point there are two possible routes:

(a) Go along the private road round the coast overlooking Loch Sunart. At several points on this road, particularly from its northmost point at Rubha Aird Earnaich, there are fines views across the loch towards the hills of Sunart. This road passes Laudale House and eventually reaches the A884 16km from Glencripesdale. It is a further 9km along this road and the A861 to Strontian.

(b) Follow the track E along the N side of the Glencripesdale Burn for 2km, then leave the burn and follow a path uphill through the forest to reach the open hillside near Lochan Dhonnachaidh. From there a forest track leads down the wooded hillside above Loch Sunart to the lochside road described above near Laudale House. Of interest are the stone benches beside the path on the way up from Glencripesdale to Lochan Dhonnachaidh; they were the resting places for those who walked this path many years ago.

225 Ardgour (Corran Ferry) to Strontian
23km/14¹/₂mls   *Maps: OS 40/46; 9*

Go SW then W for 4km by the A861 road to Sallachan. From there go W up Glen Gour, at first along the path on the S side of the River Gour. The path disappears, and about 5km up the glen cross to the N side of the river and continue to the pass between Sgurr na Laire and Sgurr nan Cnamh. From the pass go down the N side of the Strontian River for 3¹/₂km, and then follow the path which leads to the ruined cottages at Ceann a' Chreagain. Finally go SW along the track through the very fine natural woods of the Ariundle Nature Reserve to reach the road 1¹/₂km N of Strontian.

226 Strontian to Glenfinnan by Glen Hurich
31km/20mls   *Maps: OS 40/35,46; 9*

From Strontian go N by the narrow public road past Scotstown, Bellsgrove Lodge and the old lead mines. The road crosses a col at 342m and descends steeply to Kinlochan at the head of Loch Doilet. Continue NE by the forest road up the N side of Glen Hurich. The road ends just beyond Resourie bothy at the edge of the forest. From there climb steeply N then NE up the corrie between Teanga Chorrach and Meall Daimh and traverse round the head of Coire an t-Searraich to reach the Bealach an Sgriodain, where an old iron gate stands in isolation on the pass.

Descend NE down easy slopes into the head of the Cona Glen, cross the river and follow a path ENE up to the pass W of Meall nan Damh. Continue NE along the path by the Allt na Cruaiche to Callop and across the Callop River to reach the A830 road 2¹/₂km E of Glenfinnan Station.

227 Strontian to Glenfinnan by Loch Shiel
35km/22mls   *Maps: OS 40/35,46; 9*

This is an alternative to route 226. Start 1¹/₂km W of Strontian at Ardnastang, and go NE past the Free Church up a narrow road, becoming a path. In 2¹/₂km turn left up a path heading NW along the Allt nan Cailleach, cross the NE ridge of Beinn a' Chaorainn at about 400m and descend N past the disused Corantee lead mines into the forest in Coire an t-Suidhe. The path continues down the right bank of the Allt Coire an t-Suidhe to reach the narrow public road at the W end of Loch Doilet.

This point can also be reached from Strontian by following route 226 as far as Kinlochan (see above) and continuing along the road on the S side of Loch Doilet.

Continue along the road to Polloch and W for a further 1½km to the shore of Loch Shiel. The second half of this route goes NE along the forest road on the side of Loch Shiel for many kilometres. At the N end of the loch it is not feasible to cross the River Callop where it flows into the loch, so a diversion has to be made upstream for 2km to a bridge to reach the A830 road.

228 Ardgour (Aryhoulan) to Kinlochan and Strontian
25km/15½mls; 33km/20½mls   *Maps: OS 40,41/ 15,46; 9*

From Corran Ferry go 6km N along the A861 road to Aryhoulan. From there walk up the path in Glen Scaddle for 10km to the point where the glen divides in three below Sgurr Dhomhnuill. Continue along the northern glen, Gleann an Lochain Dhuibh, to the col where Lochan Dubh drains down to Glen Hurich. Go down this glen on the N side of the river to reach the end of the forest road near Resourie bothy. At this point route 226 is joined and is followed in reverse down Glen Hurich to Kinlochan and then by the narrow public road to Strontian.

An alternative to this route provides a shorter way to Strontian. From the point in Glen Scaddle where it divides in three, go up the southern glen, Gleann Mhic Phail. Its upper reaches are narrow and steep sided where the burn flows through a rocky ravine. Continue up to the col (495m) between Sgurr a' Chaorainn and Sgurr na h-Ighinn and descend steeply SW to the Strontian River where route 225 is joined and followed down to Strontian.

229 Ardgour (Aryhoulan) to Glenfinnan
26km/16mls   *Maps: OS 40,41/35,46; 9*

The start of this route is the same as the previous one. Go 6km N from Corran Ferry to the bridge over the River Scaddle and up the track on the N side of the Cona River. This track goes for about 12km nearly to the head of the Cona Glen, and from its end climb NW by a path to the col W of Meall nan Damh where route 226 is joined. Go NE by the path down the Allt na Cruaiche past Callop to the A830 road 2½km E of Glenfinnan Station.

230 Loch Moidart (Ardmolich) to Lochailort by Glen Moidart
16km/10mls   *Maps: OS 40/35,45,46; **9***

From Ardmolich at the head of Loch Moidart go up the River Moidart by road to Glenmoidart House. Continue up the glen by a path on the W side of the River Moidart. From the ruined cottage of Assary climb due N up a steep grassy slope to the Bealach an Fhiona, 705m. Traces of a path near the bealach indicate that this might once have been a more frequented route than it is nowadays. Descend steeply N from the bealach into Coire a' Bhuiridh and go down the W side of the Allt a' Bhuiridh. In due course a path appears and it leads NW then W through a little col on the S side of Tom Odhar to Glenshian Lodge Hotel and Lochailort.

231 Kilchoan (Ardnamurchan) to Acharacle
40km/25mls   *Maps: OS 40,47/45; **9,10***

Take the road from Kilchoan NW to Achnaha. From the farm track reached about 1km before Achnaha go NE by Glendrian and at 475692 go N to within 500 metres of the coast, then E to Faskadale. This section of the route is waymarked. Continue along a track to Kilmory, whence it is possible to go S by road to reach the B8007, where there is a bus service.

To continue to Acharacle go E from Kilmory by a road to Ockle, then by a track to Gortenfern, through the forest to Gorteneorn and along the S side of Kentra Bay to Arivegaig, 2km from Acharacle.

SECTION 19
Loch Eil to Glen Shiel

232 Loch Lochy (Clunes) to Loch Garry (Tomdoun)
19km/12mls   *Maps: OS 34/35,36;* **9**

Start from the car park 2½km W of Clunes at the W end of the
Dark Mile on the B8005 road. Climb steeply up the higher path on
the E side of Gleann Cia-aig through the forest and reach a forest
road. Go N along this road to its end and continue by the path which
crosses to the W side of the Abhainn Chia-aig. Continue NE along
a very faint path to Fedden, which two centuries ago was a
much-frequented drovers' stance.

At this point it is best to cross the glen NE to reach the path which
contours round below the western slopes of Sron a' Choire Ghairbh,
and follow this path NE. It enters a forested area and the route may
be difficult to follow. (If the forest becomes impenetrable, it may be
easier to go rightwards round its upper edge for a short distance).
Once the Allt Bealach Easain is reached there are no further
problems; a rough road goes down the Allt Ladaidh to join another
road which leads 3km W to Greenfield. From there go N across the
narrows of Loch Garry to the public road on the N side of the loch
4km E of Tomdoun.

233 Loch Lochy (Clunes) to Laggan Locks
16km/10mls   *Maps: 34/35,36;* **9**

(a) Follow route 232 to Fedden. From there go E across the glen
to join the path which contours round the foot of Sron a' Choire
Ghairbh. Continue E along this path, over the Cam Bhealach and
down the Allt Glas Dhoire to the forest road going NE along Loch
Lochy to Laggan Locks.

(b) A more direct, but much less interesting, alternative route
from Clunes (12km/7½mls) follows the NW shore of Loch Lochy by
the forestry road along the lochside to Laggan Locks.

234 Gairlochy to Fassfern by Glen Loy
22km/14mls   *Maps: OS 41/35;* **9**
From Gairlochy go SW by the B8004 road to Glen Loy, then up
this glen by road to Achnanellan. Continue W by an intermittent
path over the long, boggy watershed to Glensulaig cottage, and a
short distance further cross the river. The path improves and a track
leads to the forest edge where a road continues down the E side of
Gleann Suileag to Fassfern and the A830 road.

235 Kinlocheil to Strathan (Loch Arkaig)
16km/10mls   *Maps: OS 40/35;* **9**
Start from a point 2km W of Kinlocheil on the A830 road at the
foot of Gleann Fionnlighe. Go N up this glen by a good track as far
as Wauchan, and a poor track beyond there to the Allt a' Choire
Reidh, 6½km. Cross this stream by a footbridge and go N up the E
bank to its head, then climb NE and cross the pass (500m) just E of
Gualann nan Osna, the 'Panting Pass'. Descend NW down to
Gleann Camgharaidh.
Cross this glen, go up the steep hillside opposite, over the 435m
col on the SW ridge of Leac na Carnaich, and down the Allt a'
Chaorainn to the footbridge just below its junction with the River
Pean at 969907. Finally go down the river to the bridge over the
River Dessarry near Strathan, 1km W of the end of the public road
along Loch Arkaig.

236 Glenfinnan to Strathan (Loch Arkaig)
14½km/9mls   *Maps: OS 40/35;* **9**
Start from the car park on the W side of the A830 road bridge
over the River Finnan. Go up the private road on the W side of Glen
Finnan under the arches of the West Highland Railway viaduct to
Corryhully Lodge and continue past Corryhully bothy on a track
which goes for a further 1½km.
Beyond its end go NE by the narrow pass (471m) between the
steep slopes of Streap and the south side of Sgurr Thuilm, and
descend on the right bank of the Allt a' Chaorainn to the bridge over
the River Pean, where route 235 is joined for the last 1km to
Strathan.

237 Strathan (Loch Arkaig) to Morar
35km/22mls   *Maps: OS 40/34,35; 9*

(a) From Strathan at the W end of Loch Arkaig, reached by the public road from Gairlochy to a point 1km E of Strathan, cross the River Dessarry and go W along a forest road up Glen Pean for 3km and its continuation to Pean bothy at the W edge of the forest. Beyond the bothy continue along the path on the N side of the stream for 1½km into the narrow rocky upper reaches of Glen Pean, and cross to the S side of the stream before reaching Lochan Leum an t-Sagairt. Continue along the S side of the glen, cross the pass at a tiny lochan and descend to the head of Loch Morar. Go round the head of the loch to Kinlochmorar.

From there to Swordland half way along the N side of Loch Morar there is no path and the going along the lochside is very rough and slow. Any attempt to find easier going above the lochside is unlikely to be successful, though some suggestions have been made that the easiest route is along the undulating ridge 700m above the loch. At Swordland a path is reached which leads W by Brinacory to Bracorina where a road leads in a further 5km to the A830 just S of Morar. This walk may be shortened by, just before reaching Swordland, crossing the isthmus for 1km N to Tarbet on the S shore of Loch Nevis, where an infrequent ferry sails to Mallaig.

(b) An alternative route from Strathan to Kinlochmorar is up Glen Dessarry as far as the footbridge across the Allt Coire nan Uth about 5½km from Strathan, then descend SW down the burn to a bridge over the River Dessarry. This bridge can equally well be reached by a forest road from Strathan up the S side of Glen Dessarry past A'Chuil bothy. From the bridge head W then WSW into the narrow pass (no path) leading into Gleann an Lochain Eanaiche. Keep on the N side of the glen, where a path is picked up from Lochan Eanaiche to Kinlochmorar, and the preceding route is joined for the long, arduous walk to Swordland.

(c) A circular route which avoids the long walk along the N side of Loch Morar, and at the same time gives a splendid expedition into the very rough country between Morar and Knoydart, is to follow one of the above routes from Strathan to the head of Loch Morar, and the other one back again (28km).

238 Strathan (Loch Arkaig) to Inverie (Loch Nevis)
27km/17mls   *Maps: OS 40/35;* **9**

This is one of the best cross-country walks in the Western Highlands, leading through the heart of the wild mountainous country on the southern border of Knoydart. It can be combined with route 236 to give a splendid two-day expedition from Glenfinnan to Inverie, where the boat may be taken to Mallaig to get the train back to Glenfinnan. A'Chuil or Pean bothy would provide overnight shelter for this long walk.

From Strathan go NW up the N side of Glen Dessarry (as in route 237b), across the Allt Coire nan Uth and continue to the top of the pass, the Bealach an Lagain Duibh (310m), about 8km from Strathan. Continue W along a rough path on the S side of Lochan a' Mhaim in the narrow defile of the Mam na Cloich' Airde and so down to Sourlies bothy at the head of Loch Nevis. The path descending to the head of Loch Nevis has been well constructed and paved in places; it is probable that it was built at the time of the herring boom on the NW coast when Loch Nevis was an important fishing ground, and the path was used by ponies carrying barrels of herring southwards.

From Sourlies go along the shore at low tide, or over the headland at high tide, to reach the flats at the outflow of the River Carnach, and cross the river by a suspension bridge near the ruins of Carnoch village. (Boats from Mallaig and Inverie occasionally sail to Camusrory) . From Carnoch climb steeply NW by a good path to a high pass, the Mam Meadail (550m), go down Gleann Meadail and across the Inverie River to Inverie on Loch Nevis from where there is a boat service to Mallaig.

Note: This route is shown as a road on Roy's map of 1755. On the 6-inch map of 1876 it is marked as a second-class road.

239 Strathan to Tomdoun (Glen Garry)
29km/18mls   *Maps: OS 33,34/35;* **9**

From Strathan go NE up the path on the SE side of the Dearg Allt and through the pass to Kinbreack in Glen Kingie. The next problem is to cross the River Kingie to reach the paths on its N side. There is no bridge, and in wet weather or if the river is full it is very dangerous to attempt a crossing near Kinbreack, although a diversion 2km upstream might make a crossing possible. This is, therefore, not a route to be attempted if the rivers are in spate. The old right of way was on the S bank of the River Kingie, but this route is now pathless, and not recommended.

Once on the N side of the River Kingie, go down the path below Gairich for 7km to Lochan, from where there is a choice of routes:

(a) Go due N over the hill to the E end of Loch Quoich, cross by the crest of the dam and reach the road in Glen Garry 11km W of Tomdoun.

(b) From Lochan follow the Forestry Commission road which crosses the River Kingie at a bridge about 3km further downstream and then goes E over the hill just N of Lochan an Staic, and finally NE to a bridge crossing the River Garry to the road 2½km W of Tomdoun.

240 Inverie to Inverguseran and return
24km/15mls   *Maps: OS 33/34,35; 9*
Inverie is reached by a mail boat from Mallaig three days a week. Go N from the village by the road over the Mam Uidhe (140m) to Gleann na Guiserein, and down this glen to Inverguseran on the coast. To return to Inverie, go SW along the coast to Airor and then along the road going first S then SE to Inverie.

241 Inverie to Tomdoun
48km/30mls   *Maps: OS 33/34,35; 9*
This is a very long cross-country route, regardless of which of the three ways described below is followed. It ends with a long walk along Loch Quoich and down Glen Garry to reach Tomdoun, and a lift on this section would be very welcome. There is a Postbus service along this road three days a week. Depending on the route chosen, it may involve river crossings which are difficult and possibly dangerous in spate conditions. All three routes start at Inverie which is reached from Mallaig by the mail boat on three days a week.

(a) Follow route 242 over the Mam Barrisdale to the foot of Glen Barrisdale. There cross the River Barrisdale and go E up the glen right to the source of the river near Loch an Lagain Aintheich. Then go SE past that loch and down Gleann Cosaidh to Loch Quoich. Continue E for 5½km along the N shore of the loch (no path, boggy, rough going) to join the Kinlochhourn to Tomdoun road.

(b) Take the above route and 1km before reaching the bridge over the River Barrisdale turn SE up Gleann Unndalain along the path to the pass at its head (525m). Continue along the path ESE, descending gradually to lonely Lochan nam Breac, then E to the small dam at the W end of Loch Quoich. Cross the dam and go along the N shore of Loch Quoich, where there are the remains of an old track as far as the crossing of the Abhainn Cosaidh, which may be very difficult in spate.

(c) From Inverie take the route to Barrisdale for 3½km and cross the Inverie River opposite the monument (signpost). Ascend Gleann Meadail (route 238 in reverse) to the Mam Meadail pass. Descend on the E side to Carnoch and follow the River Carnach upstream on its W bank. There is an intermittent path for about 4km, but the last 2½km to Lochan nam Breac is pathless and very rough going. Join route (b) described above at Lochan nam Breac.

242 Inverie to Kinloch Hourn and Arnisdale
37km/23mls   *Maps: OS 33/35;* **9**

This is another superb long walk that combines the wild mountain scenery of Knoydart with the narrow fiord-like upper reaches of Loch Hourn.

Follow the road E up the Inverie River to Loch an Dubh- Lochain, and continue NE by the good path over the Mam Barrisdale (450m), with magnificent views towards Luinne Bheinn 1½km to the E. Go down the path to Barrisdale on Loch Hourn. From there a track goes N to a ruined house on the edge of Barrisdale Bay, and a path continues E along the S shore of Loch Hourn past Runival and Skiary to Kinloch Hourn. This point, 24km from Inverie, is at the end of the public road from Invergarry along Glen Garry, and is reached by a Postbus service three days a week.

To reach Arnisdale, cross the bridge at Kinloch Hourn, go through the grounds of Kinloch Hourn House, passing on its right into the woods behind the house, and climb steeply up a path to a pass at about 270m. 400 metres beyond the pass fork left down to the Allt a' Choire Reidh, which is crossed near Lochan Torr a' Choil. From this lochan keep NW, the path climbs a little for 1km and then descends into Gleann Dubh Lochain. Go down this glen and Glen Arnisdale to Arnisdale on the shore of Loch Hourn. If continuing to Glenelg, see route 244.

243 Kinloch Hourn to Glenelg

26km/16mls   *Maps: OS 33/35;* **9,12**

The first part of this route follows the second half of 242 from Kinloch Hourn to the path junction at 908102 in Gleann Dubh Lochain, from where there are two ways to Glenelg:

(a) Continue NW up the Allt an Tomain Odhair to the Bealach Aoidhdailean and descend NNW at first down the Allt Ghleann Aoidhdailean, on the NE side of the burn, to reach a track at the head of Gleann Beag. From that point either go down the glen by this track past Balvraid and two fine remains of Pictish brochs to reach the road beside the Sound of Sleat 1½km S of Glenelg, or go N past Suardalan bothy, cross the Glenmore River by a bridge 1/2km E of this bothy and go down Glen More to Glenelg.

The final part of this route is along the line of an Old Military Road and past the ruins of Bernera Barracks built in Hanoverian times.

(b) Alternatively, from the path junction at 908102 continue NW for only a short distance, then turn NNE up the Allt a' Choire Odhair for 1km and climb N to the Bealach Chasain, the pass between Druim na Firean and Spidean Dhomhuill Bhric. Descend NW then N along the E side of headwaters of the Glenmore River to join the previous route at the edge of the forest 1km E of Suardalan.

It is unfortunate that the pylons of the electricity transmission line from Glen Garry to Skye march alongside the route from Kinloch Hourn to Gleann Beag over the Bealach Aoidhdailean. They make it impossible to lose the way, but are totally out of sympathy with the wild landscape.

244 Glenelg to Arnisdale
12km/7½mls   *Maps: OS 33/35;* **9,12**

The shortest route goes S from Glenelg by road to Eilanreach at the bridge at the foot of Gleann Beag. From there climb due S up the pathless hillside between the Allt a' Ghearr Oir and the Allt an Fhaing, heading for the col E of Meall Bhuidhe. Once over this col, continue S to the E side of Loch na Lochain and climb SE to a tiny lochan at 360m on the Bealach Rarsaidh at the foot of the W ridge of Beinn Sgritheall. From there go S and find a path which descends steeply through the woods of Coille Mhailairigh to reach the Arnisdale road near Creag Ruadh, about 3km from the village. (This descent is rough going if the path is not found).

There have been recent reports that fences on the hillside above Eilanreach make access difficult at that point. An alternative starting point that might avoid such difficulties is on the Arnisdale road just over 1km SW of Eilanreach where there is a parking place. From there strike SE across the Allt a' Ghearr Oir to reach the route described above.

For an alternative route (19km/12mls), go up Glean Beag from Eilanreach, thus reversing route 243(a). Continue up this glen past Balvraid and go up the Allt Gleann Aoidhdailean to the Bealach Aoidhdailean (475m). There turn S round the foot of the E ridge of Beinn nan Caorach and go WSW down Coire Chorsalain and the Allt Utha (good path) to the the River Arnisdale and Arnisdale. (At the Bealach Aoidhdailean the route to Kinloch Hourn branches off – see route 243).

245 Glenelg to Shiel Bridge by Totaig
21km/13mls   *Maps: OS 33/26;* **9,12**

From the Free Church at the road fork (820199) go NW for 400 metres to the Allt Mor Ghalltair, then NE by path and track across the ridge and through a forestry plantation. Off the track and well below it (at 839237) there is a stile over a forest fence and a footbridge across the Allt na Dalach. This leads to a forest track which goes E well above the S side of Loch Alsh, rising to over 150m and then dropping down past the ruins of the broch called Caisteal Grugaig to the end of the minor road at Totaig. Finally go 7km along this road to Ratagan youth hostel and 2½km further to Shiel Bridge.

An alternative route goes round the shore from Kylerhea Ferry, joining the above route beyond Ardintoul. The path, which begins at the old ferry house, goes to the electricity transmission line and becomes a rough muddy path along the hillside, beyond which a track goes along the shore round the Garbhan Cosach promontory and along the sandy shore of Camas nan Gall to Ardintoul.

246 Kinloch Hourn to Shiel Bridge
19km/12mls   *Maps: OS 33/35;* **9,12**

Take the road from Kinloch Hourn for about 1$\frac{1}{2}$km to the N end of Loch Coire Shubh. Cross to the E bank of the stream, possibly with difficulty, and follow the path which crosses the hillside N and goes up Coire Sgoireadail to Loch Bealach Coire Sgoireadail. Descend into Wester Glen Quoich, cross the burn and climb NW to the Bealach Duibh Leac (721m), the pass between Creag nan Damh and Sgurr a' Bhac Chaolais. Descend NW from the pass down a steep slope where the zigzags of the path are rather indistinct. Lower down, after crossing the Allt Mhalagain, a good stalkers' path leads down to the A87 road in Glen Shiel, about 1km from Achnangart and 6km from Shiel Bridge.

The following alternative route is more direct (15km), but is rougher and does not follow paths as does the preceding one. Follow route 243 for 2km and take the right-hand path which crosses the Allt a' Choire Reidh and heads N towards the Allt Coire Mhalagain. When the corrie steepens, bear NE to reach the Bealach Coire Mhalagain (696m) between Sgurr na Sgine and The Saddle. From the bealach make a descending traverse NE below a dry stone dyke across rough slopes below the Forcan Ridge of The Saddle to reach the col between this ridge and Meallan Odhar. From there go NNW down the Allt a' Choire Chaoil and at its junction with the Allt a' Coire Uaine cross this burn to reach the path on its W side. Follow this path down to Shiel Bridge.

The first of these routes is marked on Roy's map of 1755. Prince Charles Edward Stewart, in his wanderings in 1746, escaped through the cordon of Hanoverian soldiers just south of Kinloch Hourn and, after hiding in Coire Sgoireadail, crossed the Bealach Duibh Leac in darkness to reach Glen Shiel where he found refuge at Achnangart.

247 Tomdoun to Shiel Bridge
37km/23mls   *Maps: OS 33,34/35;* **9,12**
    Go W from Tomdoun by road for 5km. Take the path NW up the
Allt a' Ghobhainn for about 700 metres, then leave this burn and
go N over the Mam na Seilg and NW down to the River Loyne. Cross
the river and go W along the path on the N bank. (If the river is in
spate and a crossing is not possible, then continue W along the S
side). 1km E of the watershed, the path joins a track which is
followed to Alltbeithe. There turn NW and follow another track for
2km, and continue along the path up Wester Glen Quoich to join
route 246 over the Bealach Duibh Leac to Glen Shiel.
    The walking distance can be reduced by starting from the Glen
Quoich Bridge (015041), 16km W of Tomdoun. (Postbus service
from Invergarry three days a week). From the W end of the bridge
go N by a private road alongside the loch to Alltbeithe.
    This route from Glen Loyne to Glen Quoich is shown on an 18th-
century map in the British Library as part of a route between
Aberchalder on Loch Oich and Glenelg.

248 Tomdoun to Cluanie Inn
19km/12mls   *Maps: OS 34/35;* **9**
    Take route 247 from Tomdoun to the River Loyne. Cross the
river, then go NE and up the Allt Giubhais to join the old road which
goes N then NW to Cluanie Inn.

249 Fort Augustus to Invergarry
15km/9¹/₂mls   *Maps: OS 34/36;* **9**
    Take the public road from Fort Augustus to Auchteraw and
continue SW by a forest road towards the Invervigar Burn. The
bridge shown on the 1:50,000 OS map at 336056 across this burn
has been swept away, so go W along the road on its N side. It ends
at a small stream and from there go SW through a clearing in the
forest to a gate in the boundary fence giving access to
Achadh-nan-darach bothy. Cross the Invervigar Burn by a bridge
and continue SW by a path to join a track. Follow this SW past Loch
Lundie and down the Aldernaig Burn until it enters the forest near a
small dam. At that point follow a footpath due S down to Invergarry.

SECTION 20

Glen Affric, Strathfarrar and Kintail

250 Fort Augustus to Cluanie

35¹/₂km/22mls   *Maps: OS 34/36;* **12**

From Fort Augustus go along the Auchteraw road for about 800 metres to where the Old Military Road strikes off to the right (369095) and ascends the hill in zigzags. Follow the track W up through Inchnacardoch Forest, across the Allt na Fearna about the 300m level, and in another 1¹/₂km cross the ridge and leave the forest. A short distance further the track peters out. Keeping W at 327109, cross the Allt Phocaichain (no footbridge, possibly difficult in spate) and after a short rise descend gradually to Achlain on the Glen Moriston road.

If the footpath through the forest is difficult to find, go W under the electricity transmission lines for 1km and then N down a clearing to Achlain.

From Achlain to Ceannacroc Bridge the A887 is on the line of the old road. After crossing the bridge, turn right and go up the River Doe past the Lodge, where the line of the old road (not discernible at this end) goes W over the open hillside for 7km to rejoin the A887 road at the Allt Coire Lundie on Loch Cluanie, 9km E of Cluanie Inn.

The section from the crossing of the Allt Phocaichain to Achlain and the 5¹/₂km of main road from there to Ceannacroc Bridge can be avoided by descending to Torgyle Bridge (see route 251) and then going W by the crofts on the N side of the River Moriston to a footbridge over the River Doe 400 metres N of Ceannacroc Lodge. This is probably the preferred route.

This is the Old Military Road constructed in 1750 and succeeding years. There was an old track before that time, shown on Moll's atlas of 1725; it was at that time the road to Skye, and for that reason Bernera Barracks were built at Glenelg in 1719-20. On Roy's map of 1755 the road is marked 'Great Road of Communication between Bernera and Fort Augustus'. Dr. Johnson's journey along this road from Fort Augustus to Glenelg in 1773 is described in his *Journey to the Western Islands*. He spent the night at Anoch, now Ceannacroc.

251 Fort Augustus to Tomich (Strathglass)
29km/18mls   *Maps: OS 25,26,34/27,36;* **12**
Follow route 250 from Fort Augustus as far as the crossing of the Allt Phocaichain. Continue NNW down the burn by a path which enters the forest under the electricity transmission line. A few hundred metres inside the forest a track is reached which is followed W then back NE to reach the A887 road in Glen Moriston near Torgyle Bridge.

The next section of this route, which is a right of way, has been the subject of dispute in recent years since the original path near Torgyle church was blocked by afforestation. It is hoped that this path through the forest will be re-established to lead from the church for a few hundred metres N to a point on the open hillside where a track continues under the transmission line. Go along this track over the ridge between Beinn Bhan and An Suidhe and descend past Loch na Beinne Baine well to the E of the Eas Socach. From the upper edge of the forest in Strathglass two routes are possible. One goes N down the forest road to Hilton Cottage and the road going NE by Balcladaich to Tomich. The other goes NE following the forest fence to the N side of the Allt Bail a' Chladaich, then down this burn to the forest road and thence by the farm road past Guisachan steading to Tomich.

252 Ceannacroc (Glen Moriston) to Tomich
30½km/19mls   *Maps: OS 26,34,35/27,36;* **12**
From Ceannacroc Bridge in Glen Moriston, 23km W of Invermoriston Hotel, go by Ceannacroc Lodge up the W bank of the River Doe for about 5km. Cross the river at 197135 where it is fordable in dry weather, and strike due N up the hillside to the broad col (500m) on the W of Meallan Odhar. Then descend NE down the

Allt Riabhach to enter Guisachan Forest, where a road is reached which leads to Cougie and Garve Bridge, thence by Hilton Lodge and Balcladaich to Tomich, from where a bus service goes to Cannich and Inverness.

253 Cluanie Inn to Glen Affric
24km/15mls   *Maps: OS 33,34/26,35;* **12**

From a point 1½km E of Cluanie Inn, at the W end of Loch Cluanie, go N along a track up the E bank of the Allt a' Chaorainn Mhoir for 3km. Continue N along the path through the pass and down to the River Affric. If the going is very wet, drier ground may be found by keeping higher up along the hillside.

Cross the River Affric at the bridge opposite Alltbeithe youth hostel. The public road is a further 13km down the glen, beyond the E end of Loch Affric.

An alternative route is by the stalker's path which starts 3km E of Cluanie Inn and zigzags up to Bealach Choire a' Chait (725m) which is boggy and pathless. From the bealach a path goes down Gleann na Ciche on the E side of the Allt na Ciche to reach a forest road which leads to Athnamulloch at the W end of Loch Affric. From there the end of the public road is 7km away at the other end of Loch Affric, and may be most easily reached by continuing along the forest road on the S side of the loch.

254 Corrimony (Glen Urquhart) to Tomich
10km/6mls   *Maps: OS 26/27;* **12**

Follow the A831 up Glen Urquhart and turn left across a bridge (at 394301) to Corrimony. From there a track (declared a right of way by the Court of Session in 1888) used to go SW in a direct line, keeping SE of Carn Bingally, passing Loch Caoireach and then turning W downhill to Tomich.

This track is now not used since the construction of estate and forest roads, and much of it has disappeared. An alternative from Corrimony goes SSW up the River Enrick for about 4km, where a path leads W through the forest on the S slopes of Druim na h'Aibhne, and joins another road near Loch a' Ghreidlein going downhill to Guisachan Farm near Tomich.

SCOTTISH HILL TRACKS

255 Tomich to Glen Affric

19km/12mls   *Maps: OS 25,26/26,27; 12*

(a) This is the original route westwards which fell into disuse
when the road through the Chisholm's Pass was made in the 19th
century (route 256). Cross the bridge at the SW end of Tomich
village and follow the track SW along the W bank of the Abhainn
Deabhag for 2km to a junction at 285256. (From there the original
route continues SW by Loch an Eang, but the way from there to Loch
Pollain Buidhe and beyond is now impassable). From the junction
take the track W over the hill to join the forestry road along the S
side of Loch Beinn a' Mheadhoin to the Allt Garbh, a short distance
SW of Affric Lodge.

From there the forestry road continues virtually along the old
route to Athnamulloch at the W end of Loch Affric. Cross there to
the N bank to reach the track leading to Alltbeithe youth hostel
6½km to the W. For the continuation to Kintail see route 256. 2km
before reaching the Allt Garbh there is a bridge across the river
flowing from Loch Affric which gives access in 300 metres to the
carpark at the end of the public road up Glen Affric.

(b) An alternative route is along the E bank of the Abhainn
Deabhag past Guisachan Farm, Hilton Lodge and Garve Bridge to
Cougie. Continue W over the ridge, across the Allt an Laghair and
along the hillside to the Allt Garbh, and descend the E bank of this
burn to join the forestry road described above. This route gives fine
views of the Affric hills and is recommended.

*Note: Route (a) above is the only E to W road in Ross-shire shown
on Moll's map of 1725, which marked it 'to Bealach Pass'. On Roy's
map of 1755 it is called 'Road from Kintail to Inverness', and is
shown from Tomich going by the E side of the River Glass to the
Beauly Firth. It was also known as St. Dubhthach's Pass, as St
Dubhthach in the 11th century travelled this way between his
parishes in Kintail and Tain.*

256 Cannich to Loch Duich by Glen Affric

51½km/32mls   *Maps: OS 25,26,33/26,27,35; 12*

This is a grand but very long walk, over 50km from the hotel and
youth hostel at Cannich in Strathglass to Kintail Lodge Hotel or

Ratagan youth hostel at the head of Loch Duich. It can be spread over 2 days if accommodation is available at Alltbeithe youth hostel near the head of Glen Affric or at Camban bothy in the Fionngleann.

3km SW of Cannich the Glen Affric road strikes off to the W and ascends through the beautiful Chisholm's Pass. The public road continues to within 1½km of Affric Lodge, with a carpark at its end. Walkers wishing to avoid walking along the road should cross the River Affric about 300 metres beyond the Dog Fall (7½km from Cannich) to the forest road which climbs a little and then goes along the S side of Loch Beinn a' Mheadhoin to the bridge at its W end. At that point either continue along the forest road on the S side of Loch Affric to Athnamulloch, or cross to the N side of Loch Affric and go W by the path on that side. (Do not try to cross the narrow part of Loch Affric by the footbridge at 185228). The two routes reunite just W of Athnamulloch and continue by a track to Alltbeithe youth hostel. (See route 255). Beyond the youth hostel the route divides, and there are two possibilities.

(a) One way goes W along a path on the N side of Gleann Gniomhaidh to the S end of Loch a' Bhealaich, and then climbs to the narrow pass, the Bealach an Sgairne (515m) between Beinn Fhada and A'Ghlas-bheinn. A steep descent along a good path goes down Gleann Choinneachain into Strath Croe, then a short walk leads to the road at Croe Bridge on Loch Duich, 2km NE of Kintail Lodge Hotel and 6½km from Ratagan youth hostel.

This is the original way referred to in the note to route 255. It could be linked with routes 257, 262 or 265 by following the river flowing N from Loch a' Bhealaich for 5km to the Falls of Glomach. From there a steep and narrow path leads down the W side of the great chasm of the Allt a' Ghlomaich to Glen Elchaig.

(b) An alternative route from Alltbeithe is to go SW up the Fionngleann along the path past Camban bothy. In about 5km from Alltbeithe the watershed is crossed and the path descends through the magnificent gorge of the Allt Grannda between the steep slopes of Beinn Fhada and the N ridge of Saileag. Below the gorge Gleann Lichd opens out and a track continues on the S side of the River Croe to Croe Bridge and Loch Duich.

257 Cannich to Loch Duich by Glen Cannich
58km/36mls   *Maps: OS 25,26/26,27; 12*

Go up Glen Cannich by the public road to the Loch Mullardoch dam. The reservoir has submerged most of the original lochside path, but a new path and a variety of sheep tracks have developed along the N side, in places rather rough and difficult to follow. There is a footbridge over the Allt Mullardoch and another over the Allt Taige, then a well-defined track for the next 3km to the Allt Socrach, which is bridged at a fank.

Beyond the lodge go S and round a spur about 90m above the loch and keep along the lochside to the Allt Coire Lungard and the start of a rough track leading W to Iron Lodge. Continue along this track past the mud-flats which disfigure the landscape when the water-level of the loch is low, and go along the N side of the glen to the summit (330m) close to Loch an Droma. Descend 1½km to the bridge at Iron Lodge, from where a private road goes down Glen Elchaig to Killilan. From there a narrow public road goes beside Loch Long to Loch Duich.

As an alternative to going all the way down Glen Elchaig to Loch Long, cross the River Elchaig by a footbridge about 4½km below Loch na Leitreach, then follow the S bank of the river to Camas-luinie and from there go W, climbing steeply over a pass and down the River Glennan to Bundalloch, 1½km NE of Dornie.

From the SW end of Loch na Leitreach it is possible to cross the River Elchaig and climb the steep and narrow path to the Falls of Glomach, and from there route 265 can be followed over the Bealach na Sroine to Croe Bridge and Loch Duich.

This route is shown on Roy's map of 1755 as the road from Strathglass to Plockton at the mouth of Loch Carron.

258 Glen Affric to Loch Mullardoch by Bealach Coire Ghaidheil
20km/12½mls   *Maps: OS 25/26; 12*

This is a connection between the upper reaches of Glen Affric and the head of Loch Mullardoch which might be used in conjunction with the two previous routes. From Affric Lodge take the path going W on the N side of Loch Affric, passing the head of the loch, and go up the River Affric for about 2½km to the bridge over the Allt Coire Ghaidheil. Alternatively, starting from Alltbeithe, go E for 3km to this bridge. Then go N up the stalkers' path on the E bank of the Allt Coire Ghaidheil, over the Bealach Coire Ghaidheil (715m) and down the E side of Gleann a' Choilich. Cross to the W side of the glen before reaching Loch Mullardoch, turn W above the loch and go round the mud-flats at its head to join route 257.

259 Glen Affric to Glen Cannich by the Allt Toll Easa
30km/19mls   *Maps: OS 25/27;* **12**
   Start from the car park in Glen Affric at 216242 and head up the path in Gleann nam Fiadh for 4km. Turn off NW to climb another path steeply up the Allt Toll Easa. From the pass (860m) at its head go E over Toll Creagach (1053m) and descend ESE to the col at 210280 (795m), then head NE down the slope directly towards the Loch Mullardoch dam.
   This variation of the route described in the previous edition of this book avoids the need to walk along the S side of Loch Mullardoch, where the going through the old pinewoods may be very scenic, but is also very rough and tiring. From the dam it is a further 15km down the glen to Cannich village.

260 Glen Cannich to Glen Strathfarrar
6¹/₂km/4mls   *Maps: OS 25/27;* **12**
   From Liatrie in Glen Cannich (10km W from Cannich village) go N up the Liatrie Burn, at first on the W side and then on the E side past the ruins of shielings, to reach the saddle between An Soutar and Meallan Odhar. Continue down the E side of the Allt Innis na Larach to a footbridge at 263383 over the River Farrar, 600 metres upstream from Ardchuilk, from where it is 15km down the glen to Struy. This is part of the old road from Poolewe and Wester Ross to the Corrieyairack and the south.
   The ridge here was the furthest north point on the mainland reached by Prince Charles Edward Stewart in his wanderings after Culloden. He had a rendezvous with two of his followers who had been to Poolewe to see if there was a boat waiting there to take him to France. On hearing that there was no boat, he turned south and marched over the Corrieyairack Pass to seek refuge in Prince Charlie's Cave on the south side of Ben Alder.

261 Struy (Strathglass) to Strathcarron
59½km/37mls   *Maps: OS 25,26/26,27; 12*

From Struy a private road goes for 23km up Glen Strathfarrar to the E end of Loch Monar. It is possible to drive along this road (except on Tuesdays); the key of the locked gate 1km W of Struy is kept at the cottage beside the gate (See footnote). From the Loch Monar dam continue along the N shore of the enlarged Loch Monar, the last 5km to the W end of the loch being pathless.

Continue W over the Bealach an Sgoltaidh (545m) between Bidein a' Choire Sheasgaich and Beinn Tharsuinn, and go down to Loch an Laoigh. Follow the path on its E side to Bendronaig Lodge, and continue along the track leading to Attadale for 2km. Leave the track and go W through the Bealach Alltan Ruairidh (395m), beside the small Lochan Fuara, and over undulating moorland past Loch an Fheoir to Strathcarron Hotel and station.

An alternative finish to this very long route can be made from the Bealach an Sgoltaidh by descending W to cross the Abhainn Bhearnais at the N end of Loch an Laoigh, not far from Bearnais bothy (021430). (This river crossing will not be possible in spate conditions). Climb W uphill from the head of Loch an Laoigh to reach the path which goes from Bearnais bothy to Strathcarron over 8km of wild, rocky and undulating moorland. In places the path is difficult to find, but it is fairly continuous.

Note: At the time of writing, access up the private road in Glen Strathfarrar is permitted by an agreement between the landowners and Scottish Natural Heritage. The key of the locked gate is kept at the cottage nearby, for information telephone 01463 761 260.

262 Glen Strathfarrar (Inchvuilt) to Loch Duich
49km/31mls   *Maps: OS 25/26,27; 12*

Reach Inchvuilt far up Glen Strathfarrar on foot or by car as described above for route 261. Take the private road up the Uisge Misgeach from Inchvuilt for 6km past a small power station, and continue for a further 3km along a stalker's path. Then strike NW over the col (no path) between Meallan Odhar and Meallan Buidhe to Pait Lodge on Loch Monar, fording the Allt Riabhachain about 1km S of the loch. Then turn SW below the slopes of Beinn Bheag, keeping E of several lochs. In 5km from Pait go S up the Allt Coire nan Each and past Loch Mhoicean, then SW down to Iron Lodge. From there go down Glen Elchaig to Dornie as in route 257, or over to the head of Loch Duich by route 265.

263 Struy and Glen Strathfarrar to Dornie
60km/37mls   *Maps: OS 25/26,27;* **12**
   Follow route 262 to Pait Lodge. There cross the stream and go W uphill (path indistinct and heavy going) for about 1km, then bear WSW round the foot of Meall Mor and Lurg Mhor to the N side of Loch Calavie, about 8km from Pait. Beyond the loch cross a flat col and descend E to Bendronaig Lodge. From there follow the track to Attadale for 1½km as far as the bridge over the River Ling, and go S down this river to the head of Loch Long. If the River Ling and its tributaries are in spate, it would be prudent to continue down the track to Attadale or follow the last 7km of route 261 to Strathcarron.
   It is probably best to go along the E side of the River Ling, although there is one possibly difficult crossing of a side stream after 2km. In 5km a bridge over the Allt Gleann a' Choire Dhomhain is reached from where a track leads 6km to Killilan. The last 9km from there to Dornie are along the public road beside Loch Long.

264 Struy and Glen Strathfarrar to Achnashellach
45km/28mls   *Maps: OS 25,26/26,27;* **12**
   (a) Follow route 261 to the W end of Loch Monar. Just beyond the head of the loch turn NW up the path (which peters out after 1½km) to the Bealach Bhearnais. Then go NE down another path for 2½km to a footbridge over the Allt a' Chonais. Continue down the glen and through the forest lower down by a road which reaches the A890 in Glen Carron at Craig, 4km E of Achnashellach.
   This route is marked on Roy's map of 1755 as 'Road from Loch Carron to Inverness'.
   (b) An alternative route diverges from the previous one about 10km along the N shore of Loch Monar. Go N from there up the Abhainn Srath Mhuilich past Loch Mhuilich to the col on the N side of Bidean an Eoin Deirg, then go NE down An Crom-allt (path intermittent). Near the foot of this burn turn NW to Glenuaig Lodge,

from where a track goes WSW over the watershed to the Allt a' Chonais and down the glen to Craig as in (a) above.

265 Loch Duich to the Falls of Glomach
14¹/₂km/9mls   *Maps: OS 24,25/26; 12*
      From Ratagan Youth Hostel or Kintail Lodge Hotel go round the head of Loch Duich to Croe Bridge near Morvich. Continue up Strath Croe by the road past Lienassie to Dorusduain. From there take the forest road N to the bridge over the Allt an Leoid Ghaineamhaich and continue up the path on the N side of this stream to the Bealach na Sroine (517m). Descend the path on the NE side of this pass to the River Glomach, which a short distance downstream makes a sheer drop of over 100m into a deep gorge. It is possible by scrambling carefully down a rocky path to get an excellent view of the Falls of Glomach. For the return by Glen Elchaig see routes 257 and 266.

266 Dornie to the Falls of Glomach
17¹/₂km/11mls   *Maps: OS 25,33/26; 12*
      Go along the E shore of Loch Long to Bundalloch, then by path up the bank of the River Glennan and over the pass at its head to Camas-luinie in Glen Elchaig. Continue up the S side of this glen for 2km to a footbridge at 967277, and cross the river to the private road. An alternative route is by the public road along the W shore of Loch Long to Killilan, where cars should be parked. Continue by the private road, which is a right of way, up Glen Elchaig to Loch na Leitreach. Just below this loch cross the River Elchaig by a footbridge at 009270, and continue up a path along the Allt a' Ghlomaich, which is crossed by a second footbridge. Follow the steep path for about 1¹/₂km up the west bank of the great chasm to reach the top of the Falls of Glomach. The path approaching the fall may be slippery and demands care.
      Instead of returning entirely by the same route (or by route 265), go W steeply uphill by a path from Camas-luinie and in less than 1km turn S up the Allt Mor and go SSW over the col to Coire Dhuinnid. Then go SW down the path by An Leth-allt to the old Carr Brae road, which goes high above Loch Duich to Dornie.

267 Dornie to Strathcarron Station

25km/16mls   *Maps: OS 25,33/26; **12***

Take the road along the W shore of Loch Long by Sallachy to the Nonach Lodge access road which turns left 400 metres W of the River Ling. (Cars can be taken to this point, thus reducing the length of this route by 9km). Go past the lodge up the W bank of the River Ling by a path, crossing the Allt Loch Innis nan Seangan by a footbridge close to its junction with the river. About 1km further on turn left at a ruined cottage and go N uphill, passing a small loch at the col ½km E of Loch an Iasaich.

Enter the forest and follow a track downhill for 1km to join the private road from Bendronaig Lodge to Attadale. Follow this road for 5km down to Attadale on the A890, 4km S of Strathcarron Station and Hotel.

Note: This route, with some variations, is shown on Roy's map of 1755.

268 Stromeferry to Loch Long and Dornie

22½km/14mls   *OS 24,25/26; **12***

Go from Stromeferry a few hundred metres uphill to the A890 road. On its opposite side follow a forest road S then E round the foot of Am Meallan and through the forest on the N side of Srath Ascaig for 6km to 902332, then turn S for a short distance to emerge on the S side of the forest. From there go E to reach the Allt Loch Innis nan Seangan, which is followed downhill until the path on the W side of the River Ling is reached. This path leads down to Nonach Lodge at the head of Loch Long, and the public road from there goes in a further 9km to Dornie

269 Marybank to Struy (Strathglass)

21km/13mls   *Maps: OS 26/27; **8***

From Marybank on the A832 road between Contin and Muir of Ord take the minor road S for 3km to Aultgowrie Bridge. (Alternatively, this point may be reached by road in 5km from Muir of Ord). Go uphill WSW through Achedersen on a well-defined track, ignoring the left fork after 4km, and continuing between two lochans. At the end of the track at 431486 turn S down to a footbridge over the Allt Goibhre at Tighachrochadair. Climb S for $\frac{1}{2}$km from there to join a Hydro Electric road, and follow this at first NE and E, and then S past Loch Ballach and Lochan Fada to Erchless Castle, $1\frac{1}{2}$km NE of Struy.

270 Strathpeffer to Lochluichart
22$\frac{1}{2}$km/14mls   *Maps: OS 20,26/27; **8,12***
   (a) The first part of this route from Strathpeffer can be either (i) by the road through Contin to Achilty Hotel and turn left there to Loch Achilty, or (ii) by path from Strathpeffer *via* Loch Kinellan to the Falls of Rogie, cross to the main road and go S along it for 1km then W by Craigdarroch Hotel to Loch Achilty.
   Continue W along the road on the N bank of the River Conon to the dam at the S end of Loch Luichart. From the W side of the dam a path formerly extended right along the SW side of Loch Luichart to Grudie, but it is now flooded at both ends. However, it is possible with some difficulty to follow its general line, in places quite high above the lochside, and then cross the channel which enters the head of the loch by the railway bridge 800 metres W of Loch Luichart Station to reach the A832 road.
   (b) For a longer route, follow (a) up the River Conon, and 800 metres beyond the confluence with the River Meig cross the Conon to Little Scatwell. Go up the N bank of the Meig (loch and river) to Bridgend. 500 metres further on strike NW uphill along a track through Strathconon Wood to 303567 and then fork right along a path going NNE past Loch an Eilein and on to Loch Luichart, joining route (a) about 1km E of the head of the loch.

271 Strathpeffer to Achanalt by Strathconon
30$\frac{1}{2}$km/19mls   *Maps: OS 20,25,26/27; **8,12***
   Go as in route 270(b) to Strathconon Wood and continue NW along the track for a further 2km to its end near the head of the Allt Bail a' Mhuilinn. Go N across the col to the E of Carn Garbh and descend NW to Loch Achanalt, where the path continues W to a small patch of forest and a road continues through it to a bridge over the River Bran near the A832 road 3km W of Achanalt Halt.

272 Strathconon to Achnasheen
11km/7mls   *Maps: OS 25/26,27; **12***

From Scardroy Lodge at the end of the public road in Strathconon follow the forest track NW up the Scardroy Burn. Continue over the watershed on the SW side of Carn Mhartuin and down the Allt Mhartuin to Inver and the A890 road 3km from Achnasheen.

Note: This route is marked on Roy's map of 1755 as 'Road from Loch Carron to Dingwall'. At that time there was no road via Achnasheen.

273 Marybank to Strathconon by Glen Orrin
26km/16mls   *Maps: OS 25,26/26,27; **8,12***

From Marybank take the road S for 2½km to Aultgowrie, and then go along the private road on the S side of the River Orrin for 3km. Cross the river and continue up Glen Orrin by the track on the N side for a further 5km to the dam on the Orrin Reservoir. The old path beyond that point has been submerged and there are 10km of rough walking along the N bank of the reservoir and up the River Orrin to Luipmaldrig bothy. From there go WNW up a path past Loch Airigh Lochain and over the broad ridge to descend through a small forest to Inverchoran in Strathconon.

To extend this route westwards, go 5km along the road beside Loch Beannacharain to Scardroy Lodge and from there follow route 272 to Achnasheen, a total distance from Marybank of 42km.

274 Milton (Strathconon) to Monar Lodge (Glen Strathfarrar)
24km/15mls   *Maps: OS 25,26/27; **12***

From Milton go up the Strathconon road to Inverchoran. From there take the track, then path, leading SW up Gleann Chorainn and over the col at its head to Loch na Caoidhe in the upper reaches of Glen Orrin. 1½km beyond the head of this loch cross the River Orrin and climb steeply S over the ridge NE of Druim Dubh to the head of the Allt a' Choire Dhomhain. Continue along the path down the W bank of this stream to reach Loch Monar 1½km NW of Monar Lodge. The Loch Monar dam, which can be reached by car up Glen Strathfarrar (with permission) is 1km S of the Lodge.

275 Milton (Strathconon) to Achnashellach

36km/22¹/₂mls   *Maps: OS 25,26/26,27; 12*

From Milton go up the public road in Strathconon to its end at Scardroy Lodge. (The walk may be shortened by 11km by driving to this point). Continue SW along the track to Corrievuic and onwards by the path on the N bank of the River Meig up a long and featureless glen for 12km to Glenuaig Lodge. From there a track leads over the col to the Allt a' Chonais and down this river to Craig in Glen Carron, 4km E of Achnashellach.

Looking west up Glen Strathfarrar (route 261)

The climb from Glen Carron on the way to Strathconon (route 275)

Looking towards the Cuillin across Loch Scavaig from Elgol (route 279)

SECTION 21
The Isle of Skye

276 Broadford to Kylerhea
24km/15mls   *Maps: OS 32,33/25,34,35;* **11**

From Broadford go S by the A851 road for 8km to Kinloch. There
is now extensive afforestation to the E of Kinloch and on the lower
slopes of Beinn Bhreac. The route follows a forest road which goes
SE above Kinloch Lodge Hotel. The road deteriorates to an
overgrown track along a wide break through the trees. Continue
across the lower slopes of Beinn Bhreac at a height of about 120 to
150m above sea level, with magnificent views across the Sound of
Sleat towards Beinn Sgritheall and the mountains of Knoydart.
(These views may be lost once the trees grow to their full height).
The last few kilometres of this walk go along the lower slopes of Ben
Aslak above Port Aslaig, and afforestation there is altering the
character of the hillside. It is to be hoped that this afforestation will
not obliterate the path to Kylerhea.

277 Luib to Torrin
17km/11mls   *Maps: OS 32/25;* **11**

A circular route is possible starting and finishing either at Luib or
Torrin. From Luib go S between Glas Bheinn Mhor and Beinn na
Cro past Lochain Stratha Mhoir, and down Srath Mor to the A881
road at the head of Loch Slapin. Walk along the road for 1½km to
Torrin village and take the path which starts near the church and
goes N through Srath Beag between Beinn na Cro and Beinn Dearg
Mhor. On the N side of the pass go down beside the Allt Strollamus
until, about 400 metres before reaching the A850, an old road leads
NW then W round the hillside back to Luib.

270 Sligachan to Glen Brittle
13km/8mls   *Maps: OS 32/25 or 33;* **11**

Take the A863 Glen Drynoch road for 700 metres then go SW
past Alltdearg House by a path up the NW bank of the Allt Dearg

Mor, across the Bealach a' Mhaim and down the Allt a' Mhaim to the Glen Brittle road.

Going in the reverse direction from Glen Brittle, leave the road at 424258 before reaching the first hairpin bend, cross to the forest fence and follow the path NE below the fence directly towards the Bealach a' Mhaim.

279 Sligachan to Elgol
17km/11mls   *Maps: OS 32/33;* **11**

Go up the path on the E side of the River Sligachan, over the low pass at about 85m and down Srath na Creitheach on the E side of Loch na Creitheach to reach Camasunary. Continue S by a path which goes along the E shore of Loch Scavaig, in places climbing quite high above the sea along the steep hillside of Ben Cleat.

A longer variation diverges from the route described above a very short distance S of the top of the pass at the head of Glen Sligachan. From there climb due S to cross the Druim Hain and descend past Loch a' Choire Riabhaich to the outflow of Loch Coruisk. Continue along the path SE along the rocky shore of Loch nan Leachd, which is an inner recess of Loch Scavaig. In about ½km the Bad Step must be negotiated. This involves crossing a steep rock slab by a narrow ledge just above the sea. An easier alternative is possible by climbing a gully above the slab by a fairly well marked scramble. Beyond the Bad Step the path continues easily round the point of Rubha Ban to reach Camasunary. There is no longer a bridge over the Abhainn Camas Fhionnairigh at Camasunary, and the crossing will be difficult if the stream is in spate or if the tide is high.

An alternative finish is to go E then SE from Camasunary by a rough track across the Strathaird Penninsula to reach the A881 road near Kilmarie.

280 Glen Brittle to Loch Coruisk and Sligachan
26km/16mls   *Maps: OS 32/33;* **11**

This is a difficult walk by normal standards, and should only be attempted by those with some scrambling ability. It may not be possible to cross the many streams *en route* if they are in spate, so this is also an expedition for dry conditions.

From the head of Loch Brittle take the path uphill towards Coire Lagan for about ½km, then follow a right fork across a small stream towards the foot of Sron na Ciche. Cross the Allt Coire Lagan and follow a lower path which passes below the mouth of Coir'a' Ghrunnda.

Beyond there the path is not very clear, but continue traversing at a height of about 220m ESE below Coire nan Laogh and the scress of Gars-bheinn, gradually climbing to about 280m to the tiny lochan at the source of the Allt an Fhraoich.

Once past this burn, the route turns N and continues for about 1km along a shelf, marked by cairns, as far as the Allt Coir'a' Chruidh. Cross this burn above a waterfall and continue contouring at about 300m until a large crag appears on the left. Then start descending towards the shore, crossing the Allt a' Chaoich (the Mad Burn), which may be very difficult in spate as the stream is then a foaming cascade. Go round the head of Loch na Cuilce at sea-level past the climbers' hut and along a path to the outflow of Loch Coruisk.

Cross the river by stepping stones, which may be submerged when the water level is high. Once across, the variation of route 279 is joined and followed NE by a path up the Allt a' Choire Riabhaich, over the Druim Hain and down Glen Sligachan to the Sligachan Hotel. The scenery throughout this route is magnificent.

281 Broadford to Kilbride by Boreraig and Suisnish
16km/10mls   *Maps: OS 32/25; **11***

Walk from Broadford for 2½km SW along the A881 road to within 400 metres of the old church of Cill Chriosd. Then follow the path S past Loch Lonachan and down the Allt na Pairte to Boreraig. The path passes not far from some old marble quarries, and when they were in production many years ago a narrow-gauge railway, known as the Broadford Express, ran from there to the pier at Broadford. Traces of this old railway can still be seen.

Continue W from Boreraig along the shore of Loch Eishort by a cliff path, indistinct in places, to Suisnish. From there go N along a good track to Kilbride on the A881 road near Torrin, and 6km from Broadford. This route gives superb views of the Cuillin across Loch Slapin.

282 Dunvegan to Lorgill and return
34km/21mls   *Maps: OS 23/24; **11***

This route gives a circular walk through the southern part of the Duirnish peninsula round the two prominent hills, Healabhal Mhor and Healabhal Bheag (better known as Macleod's Tables), which are the most prominent hills in this part of Skye.

The most convenient starting and finishing point is at Lonmore, 2km SE of Dunvegan at the junction of the B884 and A863 roads. Go S past Orbost to the end of the public road at the head of Loch Bharcasaig. Continue S along a track, then a path, through recently planted forest on the W side of Loch Bracadale to reach the ruins of old crofts at Idrigill. From there a path goes 1½km further S to Idrigill Point where the scenery is wild and spectacular. The three sea-stacks just off the point are Macleod's Maidens.

The route continues NW along the cliff-top for 10km to Lorgill. There is a path for most of the way, but in places the going is rough and there is a good deal of up and downhill work as the path climbs over headlands and drops down into little glens, but the scenery is always very fine.

At Lorgill the route turns inland up Gleann a' Phuill, although it is also possible to continue NNW by a rough road to Ramasaig and Borrodale. At the head of Gleann a' Phuill descend NE to Sunagill at the head of the Hamara River and reach the path which climbs below the crags of Beinn Chreagach and descends NE to Skinidin on the B884 road, 5km from Lonmore.

A shorter variation of this walk can be made by climbing from the head of Loch Bharcasaig up the E ridge of Healabhal Bheag to about 280m, where the ridge steepens towards the summit of the hill. From there traverse SW across the hillside, descending slightly to reach the Bealach Bharcasaig, and continue SW past the Ollisdal Lochs to go down Glen Ollisdal and join the cliff-top path.

SECTION 22
Wester Ross

283 Kishorn to Applecross
18km/11mls   *Maps: OS 24/25,26;* **12**

The recommended starting point (if one is arriving by car) is at 808404 on the Bealach na Ba road from Kishorn to Applecross, where there is space for car parking. From there follow a line of posts downwards for a few hundred metres, and then traverse roughly along a line of poles at about 100m above the sea to reach Airigh-drishaig. From there the best and most direct path to Toscaig goes inland past Loch Airigh Alasdair and Lochan an t-Sagairt and down near the Toscaig River. The alternative is round the coast by a poor path to Uags and then a slightly better one from there past some shielings to Toscaig.

The last part of this walk is along the normally very quiet road from Toscaig past the little villages of Camusterrach, Camusteel and Milton to Applecross. There are superb views from many points on this walk across the Inner Sound to Skye.

284 Applecross to Kenmore
16km/10mls   *Maps: OS 24/25,26;* **12**

From Applecross village go round the head of the bay and take the private road up the NW side of the River Applecross past Hartfield. Follow the road past two plantations to its end and continue along the left-hand path, which turns N and goes in an almost straight line across the desolate interior of the Applecross peninsula to Kenmore.

An alternative finish to this walk, which is about 2km shorter, is to take the right-hand path from the road-end and go NE to Inverbain.

Both these paths are old coffin routes, as cairns indicate, which were used in times past by burial parties going to the church at Applecross.

There are a few short sections of the old coastal path (now replaced by the road) which give pleasant short walks. Possibly the best of these is the old path from Cuaig to Arinacrinachd in the NW corner of the Applecross peninsula. The route is cairned, but the path is difficult to follow in places as it makes its tortuous way past several small lochans. At its NE end it is blocked by a small plantation, and one has to go round the N side to reach the road. This is a beautiful short walk, barely 5km, with wonderful views, especially if one makes a small diversion to the top of Meall Loch an Fhidhleir.

285 Lochcarron or Strathcarron to Shieldaig or Annat (Loch Torridon)

20km/12¹/₂mls   Maps: OS 24,25/26; **12**

The start of this route is on the A896 road at the head of Loch Carron, midway between Lochcarron village and Strathcarron Station. Go along the private road to Tullich Farm, and beyond there continue N up a path beside the Abhainn Bhuachaig. Cross the Bealach a' Ghlas-chnoic and descend along the N side of the Allt a' Ghiubhais.

At the point where the path turns SW towards Glasnock, leave it and cross the level glen to Ceann-loch-damh. From there two possible routes continue northwards:

(a) Cross the river flowing into Loch Damh from Loch Coultrie to reach the A896 road and follow it N to Shieldaig.

(b) Cross the Abhainn Dearg and follow the path along the E side of Loch Damh. In 4km a track is reached which continues along the lochside and reaches the A896 road midway between Shieldaig and Annat.

From that point the last few kilometres to Shieldaig go along the road. The most attractive way of reaching Annat is to cross the A896 and follow a private road down towards the little bays of Ob Gorm Beag and Ob Gorm Mor and along the wooded fringe of Loch Torridon to the Loch Torridon Hotel.

The route along the E side of Loch Damh is shown on Roy's map of 1755 as the 'road' from Lochcarron to Shieldaig, with a branch going E to the head of Loch Torridon.

286 Strathcarron to Annat (Loch Torridon) by Coulags

18km/11mls   *Maps: OS 24,25/26;* **12**

The route starts from the A890 road 4½km N from Strathcarron Station at the bridge over the Fionn-abhainn. Follow the well-defined path N past the new lodge and up the E side of the river.

In 2km the river is crossed, and in another 1km Coulags bothy is passed. 1km further on there is a junction of paths. The most direct way continues up the glen past Loch Coire Fhionnaraich to the Bealach na Lice (420m) and then down NW to Loch an Eion.

A slightly longer route, but finer scenically, is to take the left-hand path 1km N of Coulags bothy and climb W to the col at 580m between Maol Chean-dearg and Meall nan Ceapairean. Descend by the path to Loch Coire an Ruadh-staic, which is in a fine setting below the steep north face of An Ruadh-stac, and continue on a level traverse round the foot of Maol Chean-dearg to Loch an Eion, where the previous path is rejoined. From the loch there is an easy walk of 4½km down a good path to Annat at the head of Loch Torridon.

287 Achnashellach to Annat (Loch Torridon)

16km/10mls   *Maps: OS 24,25/26;* **12**

This is a very fine walk up Coire Lair in the heart of the Achnashellach mountains. Start from the A890 road at the private road leading to Achnashellach Station, go up to the station and walk along to its SW end where there is a gate giving access to a path through densely-growing rhododendrons. Follow this path uphill through fine pine woods on the N bank of the River Lair, and after leaving the forest climb more steeply towards Coire Lair, with the huge sandstone buttresses of Fuar Tholl on one's left.

In about 2½ km the path levels off and continues WNW up Coire Lair between the dark red cliffs of Sgorr Ruadh on the left and the grey quartzite screes of Beinn Liath Mhor on the right. After crossing the Bealach Coire Lair (650m) at the head of the corrie, the path drops about 100m and then continues W on a level traverse for ½km to the Bealach Ban (550m). From there the path descends SW below Meall Dearg to join route 286 on the ascent to the Bealach na Lice. Continue along that route to reach Annat.

Alternatively, one can return to Glen Carron by reversing route 286 past Coulags bothy, and thus make an almost circular walk back to the A890 road 6km from the starting point at Achnashellach.

288 Achnashellach to Kinlochewe or Glen Torridon
16km/10mls   *Maps: OS 19,25/26;* **12**
This route crosses the Coulin Pass and is the most straightforward way from Glen Carron to Glen Torridon. If one begins from Achnashellach, the descent towards Glen Torridon past Loch Coulin gives splendid views of Beinn Eighe. Start from Achnashellach Station and cross the railway to a forest road which climbs ENE for 3km to leave the forest just S of the pass. A good track continues over it and down to a bridge across the River Coulin.

An alternative way to this bridge is to follow route 287 up Coire Lair to the level part of the path at 991503. At that point take the path branching rightwards which leads NE across a col below Beinn Liath Mhor and down the Easan Dorcha to the bridge.

Continue N along the track to Coulin and turn right to cross the river to Torran-cuilinn. The direct route to Kinlochewe, and the line of the old right of way, goes NW for 200 metres, then N along a path which climbs through forest, across the SW shoulder of Carn Loisgte and down through another forest to reach Glen Torridon 2km S of Kinlochewe. This route is difficult to follow through the forest and is not recommended at present.

It is easier to continue from Torran-cuilinn along the path on the NE side of Loch Coulin to join the private road near the outflow of the loch and go along the E side of Loch Clair to reach the A896 road in Glen Torridon 5km from Kinlochewe.

The next four routes are through, or along the edge of, the splendid expanse of mountainous country between Loch Torridon and Glen Torridon on the south, and Loch Maree on the north. In this area, and particularly in its southern part, are the great Torridonian mountains, and although none of the routes described here reach their summits, they do traverse the glens between them and give wonderful views into their wild and remote corries and up towards their pinnacled ridges.

289 The Low-Level Traverse of Liathach
12km/7¹/₂mls   *Maps: OS 24,25/26; 12*

Start from the carpark 6km up Glen Torridon near Lochan an Iasgair and follow the path N through Coire Dubh Mor between the dark sandstone buttresses of Liathach and the vast scree slopes of Beinn Eighe. In about 4km the highest point of the walk is reached and the way turns W along a well reconstructed path on the N side of the string of little lochs – Lochan a' Choire Dhuibh and Loch Grobaig.

On this part of the walk there are (on a clear day) superb views of the great northern corries of Liathach, Coire na Caime in particular, backed by the high pinnacled ridge of the mountain. The path continues downhill along the Abhainn Coire Mhic Nobuill, now with Beinn Alligin's cliff-lined Toll a' Mhadaidh on the right, and finally passes through a small pine wood to reach the road between Torridon and Inveralligin.

290 Loch Torridon or Glen Torridon to Bridge of Grudie (Loch Maree)
17km/10¹/₂mls   *Maps: OS 19,24,25/26; 12*

This is another fine walk which goes through the heart of the Torridon mountains, and with a short diversion one can visit the finest of the Torridonian corries – Coire Mhic Fhearchair on Beinn Eighe.

Start from the carpark on the road between Torridon and Inveralligin at the foot of Coire Mhic Nobuill (the finishing point of route 289). Go up the path beside the Abhainn Coire Mhic Nobuill almost to the watershed near Lochan a' Choire Dhuibh, and then go E uphill for a few hundred metres to join the path which circles round the flank of Sail Mhor.

An alternative and much shorter approach to this point can be made from the carpark in Glen Torridon at the start of route 289 up the path through Coire Dubh Mor.

Follow the path round the foot of Sail Mhor and reach Loch Coire Mhic Fhearchair. Beyond the head of this lochan is the great Triple Buttress which forms the headwall of the corrie and is the most impressive example of mountain architecture in Torridon.

To continue, go back down the path for a short distance to 936613, and then follow a faint path with a few cairns downhill NNE to reach and cross the Allt Coire Mhic Fhearchair at 945630. Then follow the path down the hillside on the W of the River Grudie to Bridge of Grudie.

291 Glen Torridon to Kerrysdale (Gairloch)
20km/12¹/₂mls   *Maps: OS 19,25/19,26;* **12**

Start from the carpark in Glen Torridon as for route 289 and follow the path N through Coire Dubh Mor to Lochan a' Choire Dhuibh. From there strike N through the col between Sail Mhor and Carn na Feola, the E peak of Beinn Dearg. Go past Loch nan Cabar and the SW side of Lochan Carn na Feola, then bear NW across a very featureless tract dotted with tiny lochans to reach Poca Buidhe bothy near the head of Loch na h-Oidhche. From there follow the path along the E side of the loch and down the Abhainn a' Ghairbh Choire to reach the A832 road between Loch Maree and Kerrysdale.

An alternative finish to this walk can be made by leaving the path 1km N of the N end of Loch na h-Oidhche and going down the stream to Loch Garbhaig. From there continue downhill by the Abhainn Garbhaig and the clearing in the forest on the E side of this stream to reach the A832 road near Garbhaig House. 1km NW along the A832 road is the start of route 294 from Slattadale to Poolewe, and the addition of this walk makes a splendid cross-country route, 30km/19mls from Glen Torridon to Poolewe.

292 Loch Torridon to Shieldaig (Gairloch) by the hills
20km/12¹/₂mls   *Maps: OS 19,24/19,26;* **12**

Start as for route 290 from the Torridon to Inveralligin road at the foot of Coire Mhic Nobuill. In 1¹/₂km leave this route and follow the path N up the Allt a' Bhealaich to the Bealach a' Chomhla between Beinn Alligin and Beinn Dearg. From the cluster of lochans at the bealach bear NW on a descending traverse towards the NW end of Loch a' Bhealaich, keeping above the very rough peaty ground near the lochside. From there follow the path past Loch Gaineamhach and Loch Braigh Horrisdale to reach Shieldaig Hotel on the B8056 road 6km from Gairloch.

293 Torridon to Badachro by the coast

36km/22¹/₂mls   *Maps: OS 19,24/19,26;* **12**

This route follows the footpath round the north shore of Loch
Torridon from Torridon village to Badachro. Some sections of it can
be done along the narrow public roads at both ends, and the
distance between the road ends at Diabaig and Red Point is only
12km. Start from Torridon along the coastal path which goes below
Torridon House to Inveralligin. From there one can either walk
along the road to Diabaig, or follow the path which goes first to
Alligin Shuas and then round the rocky coast well above sea-level
to Port Laire and Diabaig.

Continue along the good footpath which goes high above the
lochside NW then N to Craig youth hostel, and from there along the
path at a lower level to Red Point where the end of the public road
is reached. Between there and Badachro it is possible to avoid the
road by following a path across the hillside to South Erradale, and
from there to Badachro by another path which goes directly past
Loch Clair. (An old 'road' in use in 1755).

It is possible to link routes 292 and 293 by striking NE from Craig
youth hostel across featureless moorland to join the path of route
292 at Loch Gaineamhach.

294 Slattadale (Loch Maree) to Poolewe

11km/7mls   *Maps: OS 19/19;* **12**

Start from the A832 road at Slattadale, 3km from the Loch Maree
Hotel. Go N along a path through the forest by the side of Loch
Maree and climb to a viewpoint overlooking the loch. Further N the
path leaves the forest and climbs NW up a glen on the S side of
Creag Mhor Thollaidh to reach a pass at 250m. Continue down a
narrow glen on the N side of the pass to reach the A832 road 2km
S of Poolewe.

The next five routes are in the Letterewe and Fisherfield forests
between Loch Maree and Loch Broom. This is one of the finest
wilderness areas in the Highlands, a region of remote mountains
and lochs, penetrated only by a few paths, some of them old rights
of way. There are no year-round habitations in the interior of this
area, and the only shelters to be found are the bothies at Carnmore

and Shenavall (which should not be used in the stalking season) so those who venture into this area should be fit, well equipped and self-reliant.

295 Kinlochewe to Poolewe
32km/20mls   *Maps: OS 19/19,26;* **12**

Go E out of Kinlochewe for ½km and turn left to Incheril. Turn left again to follow the road past several cottages, and go along the path on the N side of the Kinlochewe River to reach the head of Loch Maree. Follow the path along the loch, in places it climbs about 100m above the shore, and reach Furnace and Letterewe. From there follow the path which climbs N beside the Allt Folais, cross this stream and continue along the path for a further 1½km until it swings N towards the col at the head of Srathan Buidhe.

Leave the path and bear W, climbing to about 350m, and then go NW at this height above the steep crags of Creag Tharbh. These crags drop steeply into Loch Maree, and make any attempt to walk along the lochside very difficult. Continue above the crags for about 4km and then drop towards the lochside at Ardlair. From there follow a path to Kernsary and reach Poolewe by the private road past Inveran and along the River Ewe.

This route is the one used about 1850 by the postman travelling from Dingwall to Poolewe, as recorded by Osgood Mackenzie in his book *A Hundred Years in the Highlands.*

An alternative route between Letterewe and Kernsary is to continue along the path over the col and down Srathan Buidhe to the low ground below the NE side of Beinn Airigh Charr. Continue NW along the path, which is wet, boggy and poorly defined, past Loch an Doire Chrionach and down the Allt na Creige to Kernsary.

This is an old route to Poolewe, linking with the Coulin Pass (route 288). The alternative way described above is shown on Roy's map of 1755, and also on Arrowsmith's map of 1807.

296 Kinlochewe to Corrie Hallie (Dundonnell)
30km/19mls   *Maps: OS 19/20,26;* **12**

Go from Kinlochewe to Incheril and continue up the private road to Heights of Kinlochewe. Take the left-hand track which goes N up

Gleann na Muice, and beyond its end continue along the path up the glen to the SE end of Lochan Fada. From there bear NE towards Loch Meallan an Fhudair, beyond which the way goes N on a level traverse to the Bealach na Croise.

There is a path of sorts on the NW side of the stream flowing N from the bealach, and lower down cross to join the path on its E side. Go N along the E side of Loch an Nid and down the path beside the Abhainn Loch an Nid until it joins a track near Achnegie. Follow this track N uphill and across high moorland to Loch Coire Chaorachain, beyond which the track drops down through birch woods to reach the A832 road at Corrie Hallie, 4km from Dundonnell Hotel.

297 Poolewe to Corrie Hallie (Dundonnell)
36km/22¹/₂mls   *Maps: OS 19/19; 12*

Go up the private road along the River Ewe to Kernsary, and from there follow the path up the Allt na Creige and past Loch an Doire Chrionach, where the going is wet and boggy, to the foot of Srathan Buidhe. Continue E along the path to the head of the Fionn Loch, and across the causeway between it and the Dubh Loch. At that point one is in the heart of the Letterewe wilderness, surrounded by the great remote mountains and crags of Beinn Lair, Sgurr na Laocainn and A'Mhaighdean.

Go NE up the path past Lochan Feith Mhic-illean, across the watershed and down Gleann na Muice Beag and Gleann na Muice to Larachantivore at the foot of Beinn Dearg Mor. The crossing of Strath na Sealga to Shenavall is possibly the most problematical part of this long walk, as the two rivers – the Abhainn Gleann na Muice and more especially the Abhainn Srath na Sealga – are normally quite awkward to cross, and in spate conditions are likely to be very difficult and dangerous, if not impossible. In dry conditions a direct line from Larachantivore to Shenavall is possible, but it may be easier to cross at the point where the river flows into Loch na Sealga.

From Shenavall follow the path which climbs NE from the bothy up a little glen to reach the high moorland at the foot of Sail Liath, and continue NE to reach the track near Loch Coire Chaorachain where route 296 is joined 3km from Corrie Hallie.

298 Gruinard to Corrie Hallie (Dundonnell)
24km/15mls   *Maps: OS 19/19; 12*

Start from the A832 road 1km S of Gruinard House and go up the private road beside the Gruinard River for 9km to the boathouse at the foot of Loch na Sealga. Continue along the path on the SW side of the loch; it climbs about 30m above the level of the loch to traverse across a steep craggy hillside and from there on is easy to follow, being the remnant of an old track towards the head of the loch.

The crossing of the Abhainn Srath na Sealga may cause problems, or even be impossible if the river is in spate. At Shenavall route 297 is joined and followed NE past Loch Coire Chaorachain to Corrie Hallie.

299 Kinlochewe to Loch a' Bhraoin (Braemore)
24km/15mls   *Maps: OS 19,20/20,26; 12*

Go from Kinlochewe to Incheril and continue along the private road to Heights of Kinlochewe and take the left-hand track up Gleann na Muice, as for route 296. From the end of the track at 070667 take the path which climbs N out of the glen on its E side. In less than 2km the path forks at a small shelter; take the left-hand path N then NE for 1½km to its end at the stream high up in Gleann Tanagaidh.

Go NNE on the W side of the burn flowing down from the Bealach Gorm, and on the N side of this pass go down to the path 1½km upstream from Lochivraon bothy. Go E along this path, past the bothy and along the N shore of Loch a' Bhraoin to the ruined house at its E end. From there a track leads in 1km to the A832 road 6km from the A835 at Braemore Junction.

300 Achnasheen to Kinlochewe by Loch Fannich
25km/15½mls   *Maps: OS 19,20/26,27; 12*

Start from the A832 road 4km NE of Achnasheen at the edge of Strathbran Plantation. Follow the track which leads NE then N to the shore of Loch Fannich. (Access to this track may be barred by a high locked gate). Go W along the lochside for 2km and continue along a 'pipe track' which goes SE into Srath Chrombuill. Leave this

track at about 140637 and keep going W, gradually dropping down
to cross the Abhainn Bruachaig to find an old fence which leads to
Leckie. From there follow the track all the way down the glen past
Heights of Kinlochewe to Incheril and Kinlochewe.

301 Lochluichart to Braemore
29km/18mls   *Maps: OS 20/20,27;* **12**

Start from the A832 road 1½km W of Lochluichart station and
go up the private road beside the River Grudie to Loch Fannich and
along its N shore to Fannich Lodge. Continue along a track to the
W end of the loch and follow the path N up the Allt Leac a'
Bhealaich to the pass (550m) between Sgurr Breac and Sgurr nan
Clach Geala. Go down the path on the N side of the pass to the E
end of Loch a' Bhraoin, from where a track leads in 1km to the A832
road, 6km from its meeting with the A835 at Braemore Junction.

There is a link between routes 300 and 301 which is not shown
on the OS 1:50,000 map. Follow route 300 from the A832 to the S
side of Loch Fannich and W along the lochside for 2km. A short
distance further, at 177650, a recently made road is reached which
leads NW about ½km above the loch to the Abhainn a' Chadh
Buidhe.

On the N side of this stream leave the new road (which continues
W), follow an old grassy track round the head of Loch Fannich and
cross the Abhainn Nid to join route 301 at the foot of the Allt Leac
a' Bhealaich.

302 Dundonnell to Ullapool
10km/6mls   *Maps: OS 19/20;* **12**

Start from the A832 at Dundonnell and take the minor road
across the river to Eilean Darach. Go uphill by the road which
swings left and gradually climbs N high above the head of Little
Loch Broom. At the crest of the ridge leave the road (which
descends W to Badrallach) and follow a track NE downhill,
gradually at first then steeply to Allt na h-Airbhe (Alltnaharrie).
There is a passenger ferry from there to Ullapool, but it may not
operate in bad weather.

303 Dundonnell to the head of Loch Broom

12km/7¹/₂mls   *Maps: OS 19,20/20; 12*

From Dundonnell follow the minor road past Eilean Darach along the E side of the Dundonnell River to the bridge where it rejoins the A832. From there follow a path steeply uphill E through woods high on the N side of the Allt a' Chairn. The path climbs to 400m before passing the N end of Loch an Tiompain and descending, gradually at first then very steeply, to Inverbroom 1km S of the head of Loch Broom, and a few hundred metres from the A835 road.

SECTION 23
Easter Ross

304 Dingwall to Strathpeffer and Garve
20km/12½mls   Maps: OS 20,26/27; **8**

From Dingwall station go through the town and then due W uphill by Knockbain to the top of the ridge. Keep straight along this ridge, with Loch Ussie in a hollow on the left, to its junction with the Knock Farril ridge on the right. Then follow the track downhill and SW past Cnocmor Lodge to the main road 800 metres SW of Strathpeffer.

To continue to Garve, cross the road to the track going W by Loch Kinellan to the Falls of Rogie. From there go up the forest track on the E side of the Black Water past Rogie, then W under the railway and through the forest on the N side of Loch Garve past Strathgarve Lodge to Garve, from where one can take the train back to Dingwall.

An alternative route between Strathpeffer and Garve is by the old track shown on Roy's map of 1755. Take the road through Contin, past Loch Achilty and along the River Conon to the Loch Luichart dam. The way continues N through woods along the E side of the loch for 1km and then NE by a path over a col to reach the A832 road 1km SE of Garve. (The last part of this route is under the electricity transmission line between Loch Luichart power station and Garve).

305 Evanton to Inchbae Hotel (Garve)
28km/17mls   Maps: OS 20,21/21; **13**

From Evanton a road goes W up the N bank of the River Glass and along the SW shore of Loch Glass to Wyvis Lodge, where the road ends. Continue W up the S side of the Abhainn Beinn nan Eun for 3km, then SW up the stream flowing down from Loch Bealach Culaidh. Continue along the lochside and beyond on the line of the path which, although shown on the OS map, is not discernible on the ground. After crossing the col (near 431709) bear WSW above the forest until a gap in the plantation leads SW down to the A835 road near Inchbae Hotel, 9km from Garve. There is a bus service along this road.

306 Garve to Aultguish Inn
12km/8mls   *Maps: OS 20/21,27;* **12,13**

To avoid walking along the busy main road, leave Garve by the minor road across the Black Water, then go NW past the Home Farm to Little Garve. Cross the re-aligned A835 road at the SW end of the large cutting and climb steeply to rejoin the original path at a stile. Go NW through the forest for 2km and continue N out of the forest on the W side of Creagan an Eich Ghlais and past Lochan nam Breac. The route continues NNW across a col, drops to the Allt Bad an t-Seabhaig and then goes NW over undulating boggy ground to reach Aultguish Inn. This route was part of the old road used for carrying fish from Ullapool, as shown on Arrowsmith's map of 1807. It was superseded by the new road in 1840.

307 Aultguish Inn to Bonar Bridge
43km/27mls   *Maps: OS 20,21/20,21;* **13**

From Aultguish Inn go E along the A835 road for 2½km to Black Bridge and then N up Strath Vaich to Loch Vaich. Keep N along the E side of the loch and NE up the track which leads over a col on the E side of Meall a' Chaorainn to Deanich Lodge in Gleann Mor. Continue down this glen past Alladale Lodge and The Craigs and finally go down Strathcarron by the public road to Ardgay, 1½km from Bonar Bridge.

308 Alness to Ardgay
27km/17mls   *Maps: OS 21/21;* **13**

Leave Alness by the road up the E bank of the River Alness and in 5km, at the cross-roads at Dalnavie on the A836, turn left along the road to Ardross which then continues NW up Strath Rusdale. At Braeantra, where the public road ends, turn N alongside a wood and over Creag Braigh an t-Sratha (326m). Then go due N across the headwaters of the Wester Fearn Burn and down the E side of the burn to Garvary. Cross the burn there and go due N over Church Hill to Kincardine, 1km from Ardgay.

309 Alness to Oykell Bridge
50km/31mls   *Maps: OS 16,20,21/21; **13***

The first part of this walk is the same as route 308 as far as Braeantra. From there continue up Strath Rusdale by the private road on the N side of the Abhainn Glac an t-Seilich. Cross the col at the head of the glen to reach Lochan a' Chairn, continue along a track beside the Salachie Burn for 1½km, then W over a 437m col to Glen Calvie. Go down this glen past Glencalvie Lodge to The Craigs in Strathcarron, where route 307 is joined. There turn NW along the road past Croick and up the track in Strath Cuileannach for 8km to Lubachoinnich. 2km beyond there turn N along a path which crosses the ridge W of Cnoc nan Caorach and descends to Amat and the bridge across the River Einig 800 metres from Oykell Bridge Hotel.

310 Inverlael (Loch Broom) to Bonar Bridge
50km/31mls   *Maps: OS 20,21/20,21; **13***

This is a long and very fine walk which goes from coast to coast – Loch Broom to the Dornoch Firth – at one of the narrowest parts of Scotland. It is not a walk to be undertaken lightly as it crosses wild mountainous country to the north of Beinn Dearg. Glenbeg bothy is a possible overnight shelter.

From Inverlael (at the head of Loch Broom) go up the River Lael by the forest road to Glensguaib, and then uphill E by a path which in 2km reaches the Allt Gleann a' Mhadaidh. Continue up this glen, still heading E, past several lochans in Coire an Lochain Sgeirich, beyond which the path peters out on a broad col.

Descend SE from the col into Gleann Beag, where there is no path until the bothy at Glenbeg is reached. From the bothy go along the S side of the Abhainn a' Ghlinne Bhig for 2km to a bridge where a track starts. Follow this track down the glen to Deanich Lodge where route 307 is joined and followed down Gleann Mor past Alladale Lodge and Glencalvie Lodge to The Craigs. Finally go down the public road in Strathcarron to Ardgay and Bonar Bridge.

Alternatives: Two other ways across the mountainous western part of this route are possible, but they should only be attempted by experienced mountain walkers. Both go up the path on the N side of the River Lael SE of Glensguaib. One route turns off this path near

236834 by another path which climbs E towards Lochan a'
Chnapaich. Cross the col E of this lochan and descend by the Allt
Uisg a' Bhrisdidh to Gleann Beag.
    The other route follows the path up the River Lael to its source
at a col with some lochans. From there descend NE and follow the
stream which flows to Loch Tuath and the N end of Loch Prille, and
go NE from there across another col and down the stream on its E
side to Glenbeg bothy.

311 Inverlael to (a) Oykell Bridge and (b) Ullapool
(a) 29km/18mls; (b) 25km/16mls   Maps: OS 16,19,20/20; 13
    From Inverlael go up the River Lael for 2km (crossing to the N
side by the first bridge) and head NE out of the forest up a new track
on the W side of a deep gorge. At about 470m, above the gorge, the
ground becomes more level and the track peters out at 230875. Bear
E then NE for 3km round a hill and drop down to the old crofting
settlement of Douchary at 245902 in Glen Douchary.
    (a) A path leads down this glen along the E side of the river and
NE across the watershed to the head of Loch an Daimh. Follow the
track on the NW side of this loch past Knockdamph bothy and down
to Duag Bridge, from where a private road goes down Glen Einig to
Oykell Bridge.
    (b) To go to Ullapool, do not follow the path down Glen
Douchary, but head NW at 244903 and go round the W slopes of
Meall na Moch-eirigh to East Rhidorroch Lodge in Glen Achall.
Cross to the N side of the Rhidorroch River and go down the private
road past Loch Achall to the A835 road 1km N of Ullapool.
    Inverlael was at one time the centre of the district – Ullapool was
not founded until 1788. On Roy's map of 1755 the route going E
over the hills from Inverlael is marked 'Road from Loch Broom to
Tain'. It went over the col to the Allt na Lairige, across Glen
Douchary and NE over to Strath Mulzie, then E to Strath
Cuileannach (route 309) and down Strathcarron to the head of the
Dornoch Firth.
    Two other routes shown on the same map are (1) E from Inverlael
over the hills to Gleann Beag and Gleann Mor (route 310), and (2)
the old road to Garve, which went SE from Inverlael to the col
between Beinn Enaiglair and Iorguill, then down by Loch a'

Gharbhrain to Aultguish. The first proper road between Ullapool and Garve was made in 1792-94.

312 Ullapool to Oykell Bridge
31km/19mls   *Maps: OS 16,19,20/20,21;* **13**
   Go NW from Ullapool along the A835 road for 800 metres, then turn right up the private road on the S side of the Ullapool River, along Loch Achall and up Glen Achall to East Rhidorroch Lodge. Beyond there continue along a track which goes to Loch an Daimh, along its N shore past Knockdamph bothy and down to Duag Bridge, from where a private road leads down Glen Einig to Oykell Bridge.
   It is a further 24km to Invershin Station and Carbisdale Castle youth hostel. For Carbisdale go E on the S bank of the River Oykell from Amat, first by a track and then by the old Strath Oykell road. This route is shown as a road on Arrowsmith's map of 1807.
   An alternative route from Duag Bridge goes down Glen Einig for just over 1km, then follows a path on the right which goes E to the Allt nan Caisean. Continue SE over a col to reach the track in Strath Cuileannach, and follow it down this glen to Strathcarron and the road to Ardgay and Bonar Bridge.

313 Blughasary or Ullapool to Achiltibuie
15km/10mls or 27km/17mls   *Maps: OS 15/13 or 19;* **13**
   This is a spectacular walk, not without some difficulty, along the precipitous slopes of Ben Mor Coigach which drop steeply into the sea at the mouth of Loch Broom. The usual starting point at the E end of this walk is Blughasary (7½km due N of Ullapool). At the W end it is not necessary to walk right to Achiltibuie as the public road is reached at Culnacraig. The distance from Blughasary to Culnacraig is 8km.
   Starting from the carpark at Blughasary, follow a path WSW across grazing land for 1½km towards Camas Mor. Go through a gate in a deer fence and climb steeply almost to 200m. The path, which is fairly well marked by cairns, is quite narrow and in places exposed as it crosses the very steep rocky hillside. Some might consider the going to be more of a scramble than a walk. The path traverses a series of sandstone terraces and gradually drops down

towards the sea and is close to the shoreline below the steep slopes of Garbh Choireachan. Beyond there the path climbs again to the cottages at Culnacraig at the end of the public road. From Culnacraig there is a choice of routes, either inland by road direct to Achiltibuie or seaward by path to Achduart and then by road to Acheninver youth hostel.

For those who want to start this walk at Ullapool, the following route goes from there to Blughasary. Leave Ullapool northwards by the A835 road and ½km beyond the bridge over the Ullapool River take a path which climbs NE over the E side of Creag na Feola to join a track leading to Loch Dubh. Go round the W side of this loch to a small dam at its N end and descend from there by a track past Loch Beinn Deirg to reach Strath Kanaird. Blughasary is 1½km further on, 12km from Ullapool.

This route is shown on Arrowsmith's map of 1807 as the only way in those days from Ullapool to Achiltibuie. It is a right of way which used to be walked by the local postman.

SECTION 24
Sutherland

314 Inverkirkaig (Lochinver) to Elphin by the Fionn Loch
24km/15mls   *Maps: OS 15/13; 13*

Inverkirkaig is 5km S from Lochinver along a narrow twisting
road. Starting from there, go E along the road for 1km to the bridge
over the River Kirkaig and follow the path on the N side of the river
past the Falls of Kirkaig to the NW end of the Fionn Loch. Continue
on the path round the end of the loch and along the N side almost
as far as the SE end. Then at 144168 take a faint path which goes
ESE to Loch Gleannan a' Mhadaidh, along its N shore and in a
straight line to the Cam Loch. Half way along the N side of this loch
a path is joined which leads to the A835 road 2km from Elphin.

315 Lochinver to Elphin by Glen Canisp
23km/14½mls   *Maps: OS 15/13; 13*

Go E from Lochinver up the road to Glencanisp Lodge, and
continue along a good path up Glen Canisp, along the N side of
Loch na Gainimh and through the narrow Gleann Dhorcha to the
NW end of Lochan Fada. Cross the stream (path indistinct) and go
along the S side of this loch, then SE towards Loch a' Chroisg and S
along a low ridge to the Cam Loch. Finally go along the N side of
this loch to reach the A835 road 2km from Elphin.

316 Lochinver to Inchnadamph
24km/15mls   *Maps: OS 15/13; 13*

Go E from Lochinver up the road to Glencanisp Lodge and
follow the path up Glen Canisp as far as Suileag bothy. From there
take the path N over the moorland past Loch Crom and Loch an
Leothaid to a col just E of Cnoc an Leothaid, and descend to the
River Inver at the W end of Loch Assynt. (The A837 road is just
across the river, and the walk can be ended at this point).

To continue to Inchnadamph, go E along a path on the S side of
Loch Assynt. This path is an old right of way and follows a very

obvious dyke which makes this route unexpectedly easy to find. There is a section S of Loch a' Mhuilinn where the path disappears, but the dyke continues on the N side of the stream in the Doire Daimh, appearing as a prominent dark ridge among the surrounding lighter rocks. The path reappears and follows the dyke for about 3km and then descends to the River Loanan, passing through a gate in the deer fence at 245215. The crossing of the river may present a problem before the A837 road is reached ½km S of Inchnadamph.

317 Lochinver to Kylesku
25km/15½mls   *Maps: OS 15/13;* **13**
In order to avoid too much road walking, it is probably best to follow the first half of route 316 from Lochinver by Glen Canisp and Suileag bothy to Little Assynt at the W end of Loch Assynt. This point is 8km from Lochinver along the A837 road. From there walk for 3km NE along the A837 to Tumore.

Start the second half of this walk up the path, which is a right of way, climbing for 1½km NE to the Bealach Leireag. At that point a large cairn marks the start of the climb to the Bealach a' Chornaidh. The way is fairly obvious, but looks steep and intimidating. Higher up cairns mark the zigzag path which leads up scree and heather to the main ridge of Quinag between Spidean Coinich and Sail Gharbh.

Descend E then SE down steep grass slopes towards Lochan Bealach Cornaidh. A path develops and leads down to the N side of the loch, but it should not be followed E unless it is intended to continue in that direction to the A894 road at its highest point. To reach Kylesku bear NE from the loch down a broad sandstone ridge on the N side of the Allt na Bradhan and S of Loch nan Eun to reach the A894 road at the bridge over the burn flowing from Loch na Gainmhich. Kylesku is 5km further N along this road.

318 Altnacealgach to Inchnadamph by Ben More Assynt
20km/12½mls   *Maps: OS 15/13;* **13**
This route starts from the A837 road 4km SE of Altnacealgach Hotel. Go NE by a rough road past Loch Ailsh to Benmore Lodge, and 2½km further to the track's end beside the River Oykell.

Continue up the glen to 307173 and at that point leave the main stream, which comes down from Dubh Loch Mor, and climb N to the narrow pass between Conival and Breabag Tarsuinn. Go NW through this fine narrow defile and descend along the Allt a' Bhealaich, passing the Traligill Caves, where a good path is joined and followed down past Glenbain to Inchnadamph Hotel.

319 Kylesku to Inchnadamph by the Eas a' Chual Aluinn

16km/10mls   *Maps: OS 15/13; 13*

This is a very fine walk through the wild hinterland of the Assynt mountains, visiting one of the finest waterfalls in Scotland. The Eas a' Chual Aluinn is often said to be the highest fall in Scotland, but this may be disputed as it is not a single drop, but a series of steep cascades. In very dry weather the falls almost disappear, so they are seen at their best in wet weather or preferably just after wet weather. Either the northern or the southern half of this route can be used as an approach to the falls.

Start from the A894 road 6km S of Kylesku and follow the path round the N end of Loch na Gainmhich and uphill beside the Allt Loch Bealach a' Bhuirich to reach the Bealach a' Bhuirich. Descend steeply on its E side for 1km to a cairn at the junction in the path at the stream which flows down to the Eas a' Chual Aluinn. Take the left-hand path down this stream to the top of the falls. It is possible with care to cross the stream and follow a path further SE to get a better view of the falls.

Return to the cairn at the path junction and continue along the right-hand path for 1km to another cairn at a path junction beside two lochans at 280270. Go SW up the right-hand path to cross the col between Glas Bheinn and Beinn Uidhe, and follow the path down a long slanting traverse to Loch Fleodach Coire. Continue along a well marked line S across a flat ridge and down the Allt Poll an Droighinn to Inchnadamph Hotel.

320 Kylesku to Altnacealgach round the east side of Ben More Assynt

30km/19mls   *Maps: OS 15/13; 13*

This is an extension of the previous route which goes through some very wild and remote country on the E side of the Ben More

Assynt range. Follow route 319 to the path junction at the two little lochans at 280270. Continue along the left-hand path downhill for 3km to its end just NW of Gorm Loch Mor.

There follows a rough, pathless section for 2km along the W side of this loch to reach the continuation of the path at Loch Bealach a' Mhadaidh. This path goes SE then S round the E side of Ben More Assynt. It is quite easy to follow and goes past Loch Carn nan Conbhairean and over the shoulder of Meall an Aonaich before dropping down to Benmore Lodge where route 318 is joined and followed in reverse down to the A837 road 4km from Altnacealgach Hotel.

321 Loch Assynt to Drumbeg
11km/7mls   *Maps: OS 15/13; **13***
    The start of this route, which is a right of way, is at Tumore on the A837 road along the N side of Loch Assynt between Inchnadamph and Lochinver. From there follow the path NE for 1½km to the Bealach Leireag (260m), and descend NW down Gleann Leireag. Follow the path on the N side of the glen, and keep above the tree-line below Loch an Leothaid for the last 1km to the B869 road. Drumbeg, the only village of any size in this corner of Sutherland, is 3½km W along this road.

    If doing this route in the opposite direction, note that the start from the B869 road is marked by a large cairn 3½km E of Drumbeg.

322 Kylestrome to Achfary
11km/7mls   *Maps: OS 15/13; **13***
    From the N side of the Kylesku Bridge at Kylestrome go NE by a good track and then E along a path, climbing to about 350m. Continue NE along the path at this height above Loch an Leathaid Bhuain to the Bealach nam Fiann. Descend E and go through Achfary Forest to Lochmore Lodge, 1½km SE of Achfary.

    An alternative path goes E from Kylestrome along the N shore of Loch Glendhu and up the Maldie Burn to Loch an Leathaid Bhuain, from where it climbs N to join the route described above.

323 Kylestrome to Loch Stack
10km/6mls   *Maps: OS 9,15/13; 13*

Start from the A894 road at Duartmore Bridge 4km NW of Kylestrome. Follow a stalker's path NE across the undulating moorland past a succession of secluded lochans, reaching a height of 300m before descending past the foot of Ben Stack to reach the A838 road at Lochstack Lodge, at the NW corner of Loch Stack.

The next four routes penetrate the very remote and rugged mountains of the Reay Forest between Loch Stack and Strath More, the glen which leads from the head of Loch Hope to Altnaharra. The starting and finishing points of these routes are a long way from any villages, so the walker has to be dependent on his own transport.

324 Achfary to Strath More by the Bealach na Feithe
20km/12¹/₂mls   *Maps: OS 9/13,14; 13*

Start from the A838 road ¹/₂km N of Achfary at the bridge over the river flowing into Loch Stack. Go along the private road past Airdachuilinn to Lone cottage and continue E on the path up the grassy valley of Srath Luib na Seilich to reach the Bealach na Feithe (450m). Descend due E on the far side of the pass and reach a track which leads to Gobernuisgach Lodge at the foot of Glen Golly. From there a private road leads in a further 3km to the road in Strath More between Loch Hope and Altnaharra. The latter is the nearest hostelry, but is 15km away.

325 Achfary to Strath More by Glen Golly
24km/15mls   *Maps: OS 9/13,14; 13*

Follow route 324 for its first 3km to Lone cottage. From there continue NW by the path up the Allt Horn to the col (510m) just NW of Creagan Meall Horn. This col is at the heart of the Reay Forest mountains, surrounded by the barren, stony peaks of Foinaven, Arkle and Meall Horn. Descend the steep path E to An Dubh loch, climb a short distance and continue E to Lochan Sgeireach on the watershed at the head of Glen Golly. From there the path goes downhill for 6½km beside the Glen Golly River, which flows in a deep, birch-fringed gorge to Gobernuisgach Lodge, where route 324 is rejoined.

326 Gualin House to Strath More by Srath Dionard
25km/15½mls   *Maps: OS 9/9,14; **13***

Gualin House is remotely situated beside the A838 road between Rhiconich and Durness. This route follows a straight line which goes SE from there to Gobernuisgach Lodge through Srath Dionard, a long, deep glen hemmed in by the steep slopes of Cranstackie and the great north-eastern corries of Foinaven. Leave the road just NE of Gualin House and go up Srath Dionard by a vehicle track on the SW side of the river. (This track was made to minimise the damage being caused to the soft ground by all-terrain vehicles). Continue beyond the end of the track, picking the best way up the boggy glen, to reach Loch Dionard and go along its E shore. From the S end of the loch climb uphill along a path which leads to the top of Creag Staonsaid and drops slightly to Lochan Sgeireach where route 325 is joined and followed to Gobernuisgach Lodge.

327 Achfary to Gualin House
25km/15½mls   *Maps: OS 9/9; **13***

This route is a variation of the previous ones, combining 325 and 326, with a rough and pathless section in the middle. The first half goes from Achfary by route 325 past Lone cottage, then up the path to the col below Creagan Meall Horn and down to the outflow of An Dubh-loch. From there one has to descend by the Allt an Easain Ghil down a steep and narrow corrie to reach flat ground at the head of Loch Dionard. The second half of the route goes along the E side of this loch and down Srath Dionard, boggy and pathless at first until the track lower down the strath on the SW side of the river leads to the A838 road near Gualin House.

328 Loch Merkland to Strath More
15km/9mls   *Maps: OS 9,16/14; **13***

This is an old drove road which starts near the NW end of Loch Merkland on the A838 road from Lairg to Scourie. Follow the track which goes N along the E side of the Allt nan Albannach, then NE by the Bealach nam Meirleach between Meall a' Chleirich and a chain of three small lochs. Continue along the track down the glen of the Allt a' Chraois to Gobernuisgach Lodge and the road in Strath More.

The next two routes cross the vast tract of undulating moorland of the Ben Armine Forest on the eastern border of Sutherland. This is a part of Northern Scotland which is in complete contrast with the mountainous Northwest Highlands described in the preceding pages.

329 Lairg to Crask by Loch Choire
37km/23mls   *Maps: OS 16/14; 13*
Go along the road from Lairg to Tongue for 8km to the start of a moorland track 1km beyond Dalmichy. Follow this track E to Dalnessie far up the River Brora, then go upstream for 3½km to a fork in the stream and the track. Follow the left-hand track up the Allt Gobhlach and keep going N over a boggy col and down the E bank of the Allt Coire na Fearna to the head of Loch Choire. Turn W and follow the path along the N shore of Loch a' Bhealaich, through the Bealach Easach and over a col to descend W down Srath a' Chraisg to Crask Inn.

330 Crask to Kinbrace
40km/25mls   *Maps: OS 16,17/14,15; 13*
From Crask Inn reverse the last part of route 329 through the Bealach Easach to Loch a' Bhealaich and Loch Choire. Continue along the lochside to Loch Choire Lodge, and then go E along a private road to Gearnsary and past Loch an Alltan Fhearna and the S end of Loch Badanloch to the B871 road 6km W of Kinbrace, where there is a station with a rather infrequent train service.

Index

NOTE

The **Map Coverage Diagram**
and **Route Map Notes**
will be found at the end of the
Map Section for easy reference.

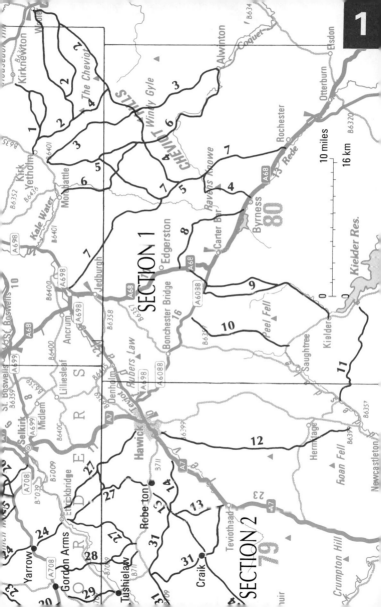

SECTION 1

SECTION 2

Kirknewton
Kirk Yetholm
Morebattle
Jedburgh
St. Boswells
Ancrum
Lilliesleaf
Midlem
Selkirk
Denholm
Hawick
Bonchester Bridge
Edgerston
Byrness
Rochester
Otterburn
Elsdon
Alwinton
Carter Bar
Kielder
Saughtree
Hermitage
Newcastleton
Teviothead
Craik
Tushielaw
Gordon Arms
Yarrow
Ettrickbridge
Roberton

The Cheviot
CHEVIOT HILLS
Windy Gyle
Ravens Knowe
Peel Fell
Faan Fell
Crumpton Hill
Rubers Law
Kale Water
Kielder Res.
Rede

10 miles
16 km

80
79

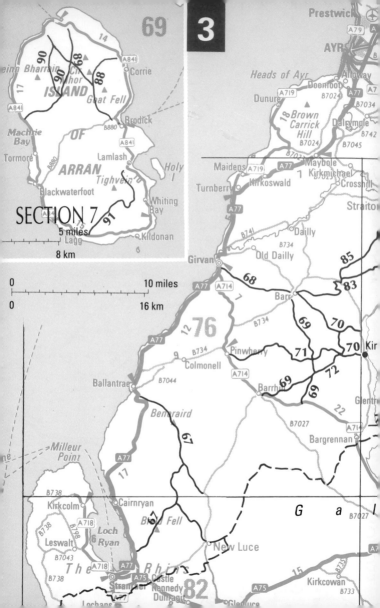

Prestwick

A79

AYR

Heads of Ayr

Doonfoot

Alloway

B7024

A77

A7

Dunure

A719

B7034

18 Brown
Carrick
Hill

Dalrymple

B742

B7024

B7045

14

A841

Corrie

einn Bharrain

90

89

90

88

Ch
hor

17

ISLAND

Goat Fell

Brodick

B880

OF

A841

Machrie
Bay

ARRAN

Lamlash

Tormore

B880

Tighvein

Holy
I

Maidens

A719

A77

Maybole

1

Kirkmichael

Blackwaterfoot

SECTION 7

Whiting
Bay

Turnberry

Kirkoswald

Crosshill

A77

Straiton

91

5 miles

Kildonan

B741

Dailly

8 km

Lagg

Old Dailly

B734

85

Girvan

0

10 miles

A77

A714

68

Barr

83

0

16 km

12

76

B734

69

70

A77

9

B734

Pinwherry

71

70 Kir

Colmonell

A714

72

Ballantrae

B7044

Barrhill

69

Glentr

Benaraird

67

B7027

69

22

A714

Bargrennan

Milleur
Point

A77

17

ne

G   a   l

B7027

Kirkcolm

Cairnryan

B738

Bla   Fell

A718

B738

A77

Loch
6 Ryan

New Luce

A7

Leswalt

B7043

B738

The

A718

Rhi

A75

A75

Kirkcowan

B733

A75

Castle
Kennedy

82

Stran

Dumfagit

Lochans

Gledure

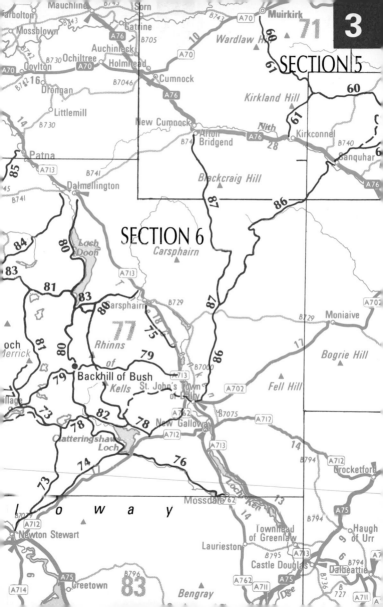

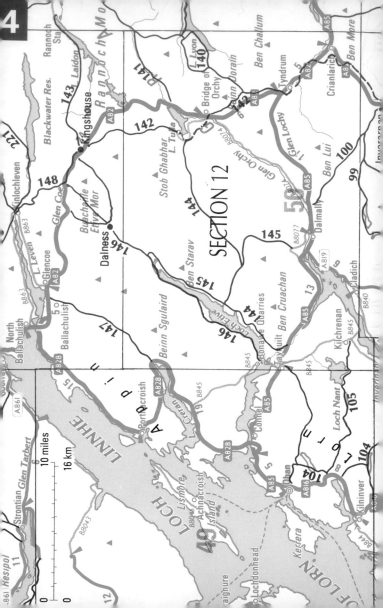

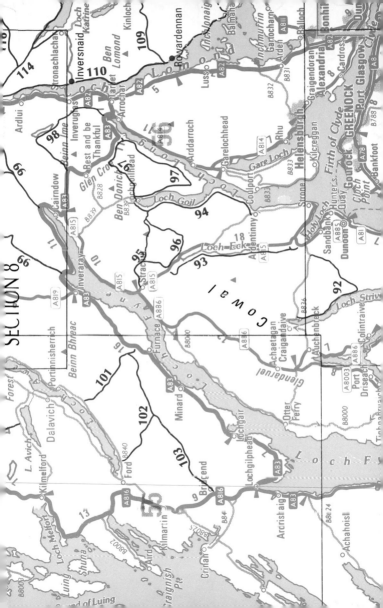

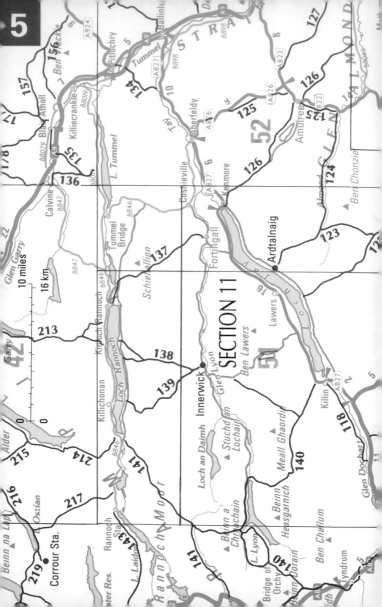

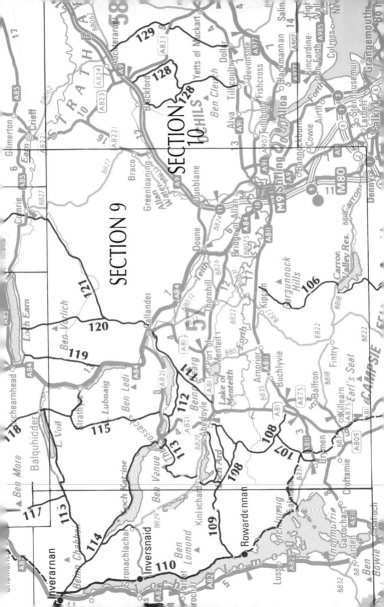

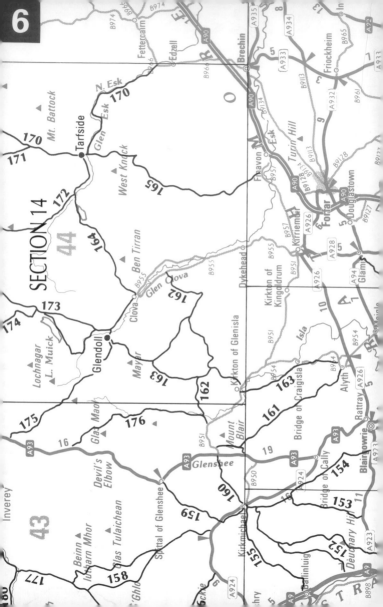

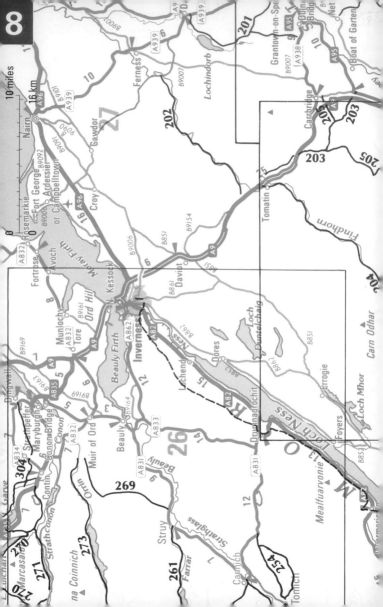

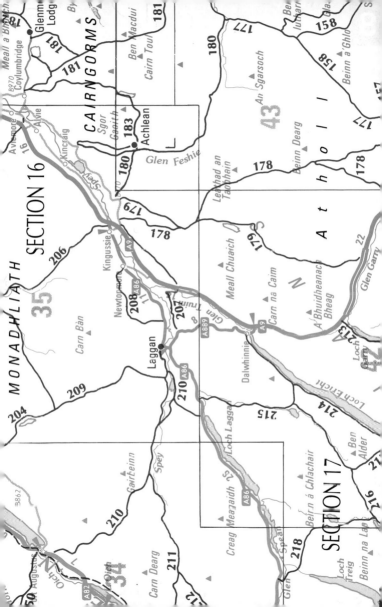

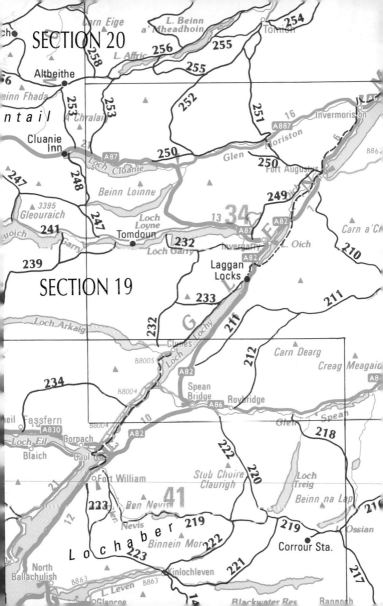

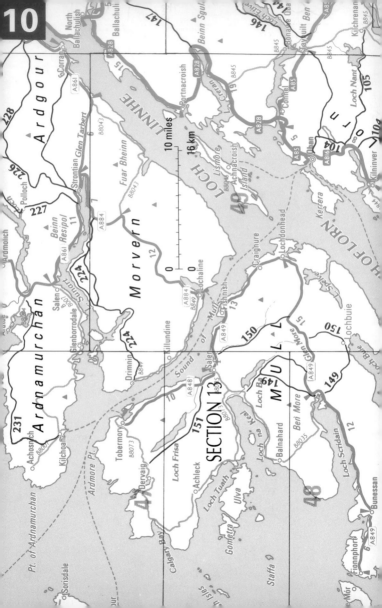

10

SECTION 13

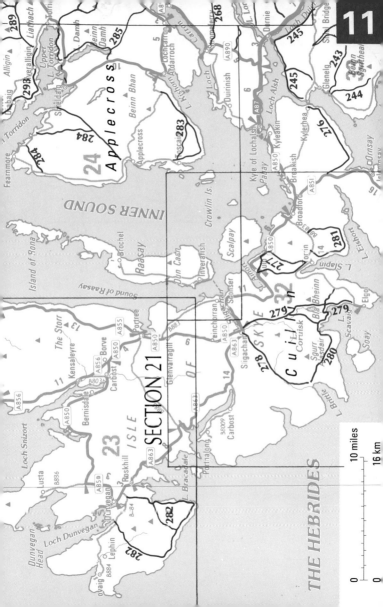

THE HEBRIDES

SECTION 21

ISLE OF SKYE

Cuillin

Applecross

INNER SOUND

Island of Rona

Raasay

Sound of Raasay

Dunvegan Head

Loch Dunvegan

Loch Snizort

The Storr

289
285
268
245
243
300
244
245
279
293
283
284
284
281
277
279
292
278
280
282
24
32
23
13
11

Liathach
Alligin
Upper L. Torridon
Diabaig
Fearnmore
Beinn Damh
Beinn Eighe
Carron
L. Carron
Lochcarron
Ardarroch
Beinn Bhan
Applecross
Ascaig
Duirinish
L. Kishorn
Dornie
L. Long
Loch Duich
Shiel Bridge
Glenelg
Beinn Sgritheall
Ornsay
L. Alsh
Kyle of Lochalsh
Kyleakin
Kylerhea
Broadford
Paty
Beinn na Caillich
L. Eishort
L. Slapin
Blaven
Bla Bheinn
Sgurr na Coirisk
Sgurr Alasdair
Scavaig
Soay
Eigol
Crowlin Is.
Scalpay
Sconser
Sligachan
Feinchbran
Glamaig
Portree
Borve
Carbost
Kensaleyre
Bernisdale
Edinbane
Roskhill
Dunvegan
Lephin
Struan
Bracadale
Carbost
Portnalong
L. Brittle
L. Scavaig
Luib
Lusta
Elgol

Brochel
Dun Caan
Inverarish

A8
A890
A87
A87
A890
A851
A850
A830
A863
A863
A863
A863
A855
A850
A856
A850
A8036
B8036
A850
A856
A850
B884
B886
B883
B884
B-84

0   10 miles
0   16 km

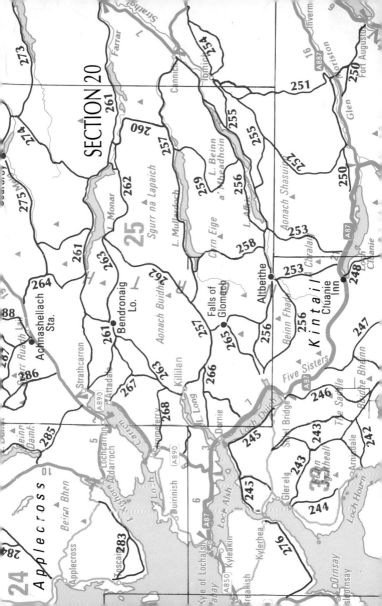

Bettyhill

Borgie

Tongue

12

Kyle of Tongue

11

Kinbrace

Strathnaver

B871

B871

B871

Syre

B873

Loch Loyal

Loch Loyal

Ben Loyal

L. Rimsdale

330

Creag Mhòr

Loch Naver

Ben Klibreck

L. Choire

329

(A836)

B873

Strath Vagastie

329

329

16

A836

Altnaharra

20

Crask Inn

21

Shinness

A838

Loch Shin

Loch Hope

Ben Hope

Strath More

Ben Hee

328

SECTION 24

A838

18

Loch Eriboll

Cranstackie

325

324

Loch Stack

Loch More

A838

9

14

326

327

Rhiconich Foinaven

325

16

S

320

319

319

Inchnadamph Ben More Assynt

A837

318

A837

9

8

Achúaisgill

B801

Laxford Bridge

A838

Achfary

322

Kylestrome

Unapool

319

317

(A894)

A837

N

315

Kinlochbervie

Lochinchard

Loch Laxford

A894

323

10

A894

B869

Quinag

327

Loch Assynt

316

15

L. 314

A837

Scourie

Handa I.

Oldany I. Eddrachillis Bay

Drumbeg

315

315

Lochinver

Loch Sionascaig

Cul Mòr

10 miles

16 km

Kinlochbervie

Clashnessie Stoer

Pt. of Stoer

Clachtoll

B869

Loch Inver

Enard Bay

0

0

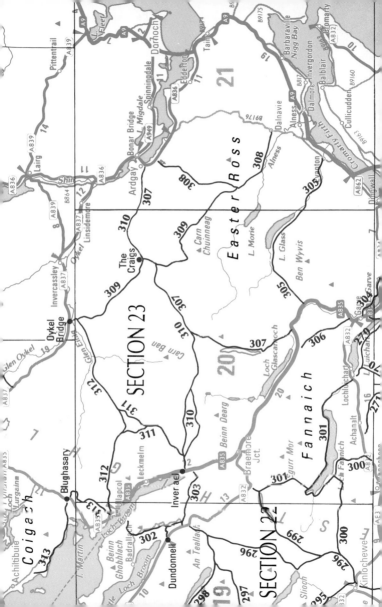

Map Coverage Diagram

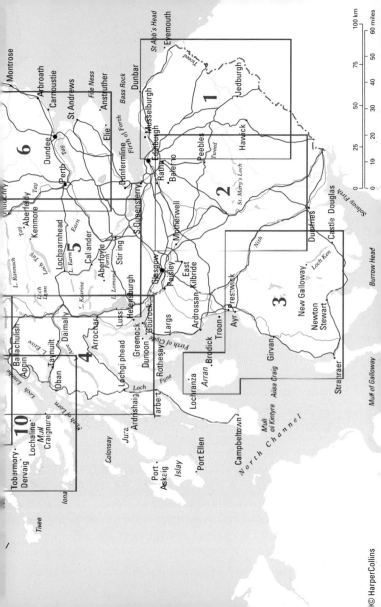

© HarperCollins

SCOTTISH HILL TRACKS

Key to Route Map Section:

21	Route (with number)
— — —	Long Distance Path
43	OS 1:50,000 (40x40km square)

Note: OS sheet numbers are also shown above each route entry, thus: **1:50,000** (before) / **One-inch** (after).
For 6-figure map references, first 3 figures read W-E, second 3 figures read S-N

Knoydart	Local area
Strathan	Route locality
Forres	Destination (off map)

Scale 1:450,000

0		5		10		15 miles	(1 inch to 7 miles)
0	5	10	15	20	25 km		(1 cm to 4.5 km)

except maps **10**, **11** and **13** (1 inch to 8 miles / 1 cm to 5.1 km)

Other communications are shown on the base map (grey) with numbered classified roads and selected minor roads.

Base map: © HarperCollins*Publishers*,
based upon Ordnance Survey maps with the permission of The Controller of HMSO. © Crown Copyright 1995.

Routes compiled by John Bartholomew and drawn by David Langworth.